A Parent's Guide to
Sports Nutrition
for Young Athletes

By

Bunny Foxhoven, R.D.

This book is a compilation of the most current scientific research. Author is not responsible for changes in common knowledge or variations in your child's nutrition needs.

© 2003 by Bunny Foxhoven, R.D. All rights reserved.

No part of this book may be reproduced, stored in a retrieval system, or transmitted by any means, electronic, mechanical, photocopying, recording, or otherwise, without written permission from the author.

ISBN: 1-4107-4302-0 (e-book)
ISBN: 1-4107-4301-2 (Paperback)

This book is printed on acid free paper.

1stBooks - rev. 07/28/03

Dedication

For my husband Brian and my children
Danielle and Zack
Thanks for all of your support and the
hours of entertainment I have had watching you play!

A Parent's Guide to Sports Nutrition for Young Athletes

Introduction

Parents often come to me asking how to get their kids to eat better. What should they eat before games, what are the best choices for snacks and how do parents stop their kids from wanting so much unhealthy food. There is so much advertising directed at children for sweets, soda and fast foods, children find it difficult not to want the junk food. At the weekend games the concession stands sell frozen, colored sugar water, candy bars and hot dogs, and then I see players holding their sides on the sidelines of their games gasping from stomach cramps!

Like adults, children need good nutrition for maintaining good health and improving athletic performance. In addition, nutrition must provide for physical growth and development. This book will focus on the nutritional issues specific to growing athletes: fluids and electrolytes; protein; carbohydrates; fat; vitamins; minerals; and other factors involved in athletics.

This Nutrition book has been designed to help you plan and prepare nutritious meals for your kids during weekly practices, games, tournaments, travel and every day life! The four purposes of this book are to:

1. teach parents and children the importance of making good nutrition choices for growth, energy and performance;
2. help parents understand their children's need for carbohydrates, protein, fat, vitamins, minerals and water;
3. introduce and encourage good daily eating habits, giving kids every opportunity to perform at their highest level;
4. provide ideas, recipes and shopping tips for making these choices easier;

As you will see, the book has been divided into three parts. Part One contains nutrition information and research specific to growing athletes. Part Two lists good food choices for breakfasts, lunches, dinners, snacks and sports drinks. It also outlines the optimal timing of meals and snacks (when to eat). Part Three has recipes and fun ideas that your kids will love This will assist you in making healthy foods available for them.

When considering the nutrition needs of your kids, keep the following tips in mind:

- Young athletes are ALL unique in their energy needs. Their sports can require both endurance and short bursts of high-intensity energy. Feed them accordingly!

- Human bodies are like engines.. if you put bad fuel in the engines, they won't run well!

- Your child athletes are still, growing, calorie-burning machines. There will be times when they *can't* get enough to eat as well as times when they aren't very hungry. Teach them how to listen to their bodies and eat accordingly. These athletes need carbohydrates, protein and fat. Be aware that diets that restrict carbohydrates <u>*ARE NOT*</u> recommended for most athletes.

- ***Timing of meals is extremely important.*** Be conscious of this during meal planning time. Begin experimenting several weeks prior to the start of the first game to determine which foods work best and how much time in advance they need to be eaten to be most effective. Tournament time is not the time to begin experimenting with your diet.

The Food Guide Pyramid created by the United States Department of Agriculture and the U.S. Department of Health and Human Services is a good guideline for how to balance your diet. I have altered the position of the food groups to reflect the special needs of athletes. Use it as a reference. I have included a copy in this guide with tips on how to use it. This will help you choose a wide variety of foods from all of the food groups. The pyramid also lists recommended portion sizes to ensure that the athletes are eating the right amounts.

Try to base your nutrition plan on these ***three important keys*** to healthy eating:

1. Provide healthy foods such as whole grain breads instead of white breads, deli meats instead of processed luncheon meats, and fresh fruits and vegetables in place of canned or processed ones.

2. Offer a wide variety of foods. Eating from all the food groups provides the vitamins and minerals that your body needs for performance.

3. Limit the amount of "junk food" (candy, soda, desserts, sweets, chips, ice cream, etc.) in your kitchen. Kids will eat much less junk if its not around! Encourage them not to consume any junk food near game time or prior to training.

I hope this book helps you provide the most nutritious foods for your athletes and helps them on their road to success.

Thank you and good luck!

Sincerely,

Bunny Foxhoven, RD

Part One

Nutrition Basics

Chapter 1 1

A Healthy Start

Chapter 2 3

Hydration

Chapter 3 7

Food Guide Pyramid

Chapter 4 12

Energy Sources from Food

Chapter 5 16

Carbohydrates

Chapter 6 24

Glycemic Index

Chapter 7 27

Best Carbohydrate choices

Chapter 8 30

Protein and Amino Acids

Chapter 9 35

Best Protein Choices

Chapter 10 37

Fat

Chapter 11 42

Cholesterol

Chapter 12 44

Calculating your child's calorie needs

Chapter 13 51

Vitamins And Minerals

Chapter 1

A Healthy Start

Food is one of life's pleasures. It is important for fueling the body, providing vitamins, minerals and fiber, and giving you energy to perform your best. It contains the basic nutrients to help you perform. There are 6 basic types of nutrients in foods.

Water is perhaps the most important nutrient. It makes up between 60% - 75% of our body weight. It stabilizes body temperature, carries nutrients to and wastes away from cells, and is needed for all cellular functions. Athletes especially need water for optimal performance.

Carbohydrates (carbs) are the primary source of fuel for our muscles and brain. They come from fruits, vegetables, grains, and dairy products. Athletes should eat about 60% of their total daily calories from carbs.

Protein is essential for building and repairing muscles, red blood cells and other tissues, and to some extent, it is used for energy. Protein should be eaten primarily after a workout, but small amounts can be eaten before a workout. About 15% of your total daily calories should come from protein foods such as meat, fish, poultry, eggs, beans and dairy products.

Fat is a source of stored energy that is burned during low intensity exercises. It is best eaten at least 4 hours before a game

Bunny Foxhoven, R.D.

and/or with the post-game meal. Athletes should eat about 25% of their total daily calories from fats.

Vitamins are chemicals which allow your body to utilize food. The primary vitamins are: vitamin A, B complex, C, D, E, and K. Vitamins are found in a wide variety of foods.

Minerals are elements that form the structures of the body. For example, calcium is needed for bones and iron for red blood cells. Minerals are also found in a wide variety of foods.

We will discuss each one of theses vital nutrients in greater detail throughout this book.

Chapter 2

Hydration

Water is the most important nutrient for athletes. The human body can survive up to a month without food but can only survive a few days without water . Drinking too little water and sweating too much leads to over-heating, decreased performance, mental and physical fatigue and possibly even death. Athletes, especially kids, need to learn how to pre-hydrate, drink while exercising, and then replace all of the lost fluids after every game or practice session. The athlete must drink enough to get back into water balance.

During various activities, children use more energy per pound of body weight than adults do, possibly as much as 25 % to 30% more. Thus kids produce more heat during exercise than adults due to the higher energy cost of performing the exercise. (1) If this heat is not quickly removed from the body, the core temperature of the body will continue to rise leading to poor performance, slower mental functioning and rapid fatigue. Evaporation of sweat is the body's main method of cooling off, particularly in hot weather. While sweating is an efficient method of cooling down, it may result in excessive loss of body fluid and many necessary electrolytes such as sodium and potassium. To prevent this overheating, athletes must be sure to drink enough to replace all of the lost fluids and electrolytes.

Unfortunately, thirst is a poor indicator of hydration because it kicks in too late and isn't very accurate. As a matter of fact, you may lose up to 2% of your body fluids before you even become thirsty. Research has shown that losing as little as 2% of total body fluids can: impair the body's ability to regulate temperature, reduces endurance and aerobic performance and increases the risk of heat injury. Body fluid loss of 4% - 10 % leads to a decrease in muscular strength, power and endurance. A loss of greater than 10% is serious can result in heat stroke, heat exhaustion, and even death! (2)

Voluntary dehydration (when a person chooses to become dehydrated for reasons such as "making weight" or "having a full stomach") can have a serious effect on performance and health. Teach your young athletes the dangers of being dehydrated and stress the importance of drinking frequently even when they may not feel thirsty.

Many kids as well as adults will find it easier to drink a flavored beverage than plain water.(3) Much research has gone into creating sports drinks that taste good and provide the proper calorie and electrolyte balance to help athletes stay hydrated. The best sports drink for your child is the one that they like and will drink the most often! Experiment ahead of time and find the one that they enjoy the most and works the best for their performance. Soda and juice are not good hydrators because they contain too much sugar and may end up causing stomach cramping and bloating, especially if used too soon before exercise.

The simplest way to determine if your child athlete is drinking enough water is to have him or her monitor their urine. If the urine is dark yellow or if the child isn't needing to use the restroom regularly, he or she may be dehydrated. Teach your child to drink enough to keep their urine pale yellow. Another way to determine fluid loss is to have them weigh themselves before and after a workout. They need to drink 16- 24 ounces of fluid for every pound they lose. Remember, some kids sweat more than others; therefore, they need to drink more to stay hydrated.

Studies have shown that people will drink more fluids if the beverages are cold rather than room temperature. (1) Drinking cooler water may also aid in bringing down the body's core temperature and improving performance. It is a good idea to purchase a large enough water bottle to hold adequate amounts of water and which has an opening large enough to fit ice cubes. Also pack a cooler full of water bottles, sports drinks and plenty of ice for all day events. (4)

Thirst is not a good indicator of hydration. It kicks in AFTER dehydration has already set in. This may be too late. Here are some general guidelines to teach your athletes about staying hydrated: (5,1)

Pre-hydration:

1. Drink at least 16 ounces of water when waking up in the morning.
2. Drink at least 16 ounces of water or sports drink 2 hours prior to game time.
3. Drink another 4 to 8 ounces (1/4 to 1/2 of a 16 oz. water bottle) 10 minutes prior to game time.

During training or game hydration:

1. Have your kids weigh themselves prior to practice and again after practice to see how much water weight is lost during practice. Have them drink enough to replace the lost weight.
2. Teach them to drink as much as possible, as often as possible, during the game. Show them how much they need to drink to replace their lost sweat.
3. In hot weather, they need to drink even more!
4. Use a sports drink if they sweat a lot, if they will be exercising longer than 90 minutes, or if the taste makes them want to drink more.

Post training/game hydration:

1. Weigh yourself after the game to see how much water weight was lost. Drink enough to replace the weight lost.
2. Drink enough throughout the day to stay hydrated and ready for the next workout.

Bunny Foxhoven, R.D.

Table 1 below shows how much athletes should drink daily based on their weight.

Athletes Weight in pounds	Ounces to drink daily	Ounces to drink during games
50 to 75	25 to 36	16 to 20
76 to 100	37 to 50	16 to 24
101 to 125	50 to 62	20 to 30
126 to 150	63 to 75	24 to 32
151 and up	75 or more (calculate .5 oz/lb weight)	32 or more

Information compiled from references 3,4, and 5

Remember that staying hydrated is one of the most important things an athlete can do to stay healthy and perform at the highest level possible. Encourage and teach your child to drink plenty.

Chapter 3

Food Guide Pyramid

The Food Guide Pyramid was created by the United States Department of Agriculture and the United States Department of Health and Human Services to help people understand the importance of eating a well-balanced, healthy diet. It is a great tool to help you plan and prepare nutritious meals for your family. Athletes, however, have increased needs for complex carbohydrates, protein, calories, vitamins, minerals and water. Therefore, I have made a few modifications in the Food Guide Pyramid for this book to emphasize the importance of meeting these increased needs for your young athlete.

I have included both a copy of the original Food Guide Pyramid and I have created my own "Food Power Tower" which I feel better defines the nutritional needs of child athletes. This will help you buy and plan nutritious meals for your kids. When doing this, be sure to include a wide variety of foods from all of the food groups to ensure that your children have the opportunity to get all of the nutrients they need.

Listed below are the specific changes I have made from the Food Guide Pyramid to the Food Power Tower for child athletes:

Bunny Foxhoven, R.D.

Change #1

As illustrated in the food guide pyramid, carbohydrates make up the base. I have replaced the grain group that was at the bottom of the food guide pyramid with the fruit and vegetable group in the food power tower. This emphasizes the importance of fruits and vegetables in the athletes diet. Fruits and vegetables provide carbohydrates for energy, vitamins, minerals and fiber.

Change # 2

The grain group also provides wonderful sources of carbohydrates for energy and recovery. Thus I have moved the grains to the next block up in the Food Power Tower and placed a heavy emphasis on the "complex" carbohydrates such as whole grain breads, pastas, and cereals. I have also removed the refined starches and sugars and put them in the top of the tower for occasional use. Foods in this group include white bread, instant rice, sugary cereals and pastries. Athletes should be eating at least 55% or more of their calories from the fruit, vegetable and whole grain groups. Eating foods from these complex-carbohydrate containing groups will ensure that your child athletes are getting plenty of energy-supplying foods for their exercise.

Change #3

The protein/meat group provides the necessary protein for muscle building, growth and exercise recovery. I have moved this group to occupy a larger area of the tower to emphasize the fact that athletes need more protein than non athletes. Foods in this group also provide many other vitamins and minerals that are not found in the other food groups. In the protein/meat group you will see foods such as meat, poultry, fish, eggs and game meats. Vegetarian sources of protein such as tofu, textured vegetable proteins products (t.v.p.), soy products, nuts, beans and other legumes are also in this group. Protein should make up approximately 20% of the daily calories. I have included a chart and a few simple formulas to help you figure out your childs protein needs in chapter 8.

Change#4

The dairy group provides both protein and carbohydrates, as well as many important vitamins and minerals. I have combined it with the foods in the protein/meat group to show that foods in the dairy group can be interchanged with foods in the protein group. However, growing kids need to get at least 4 good sources of calcium daily, which is primarily found in dairy foods. Foods that are fortified with calcium, such as soy milk/cheeses, calcium fortified juices and many green leafy vegetables, can also supply a good portion of the daily calcium needs.

Change #5

I have placed several blocks of foods in the top of the Food Power Tower to show that it is OK for kids to have a small amounts of these "junk food" occasionally! It's OK to have some pizza, cookies or other "junk food" here and there just not too often. Be sure that the foods in the top boxes of the tower do not interfere with other healthier food choices!

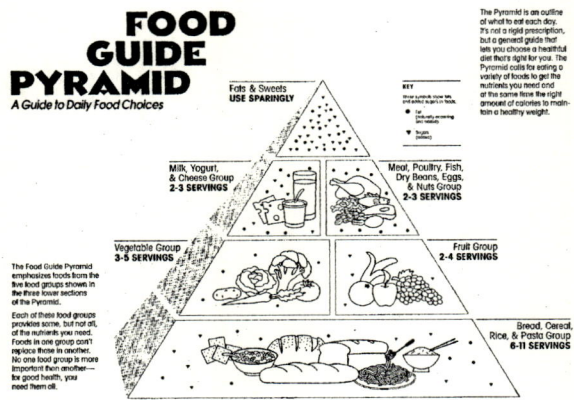

Figure 1. USDA Food Guide Pyramid before any modifications

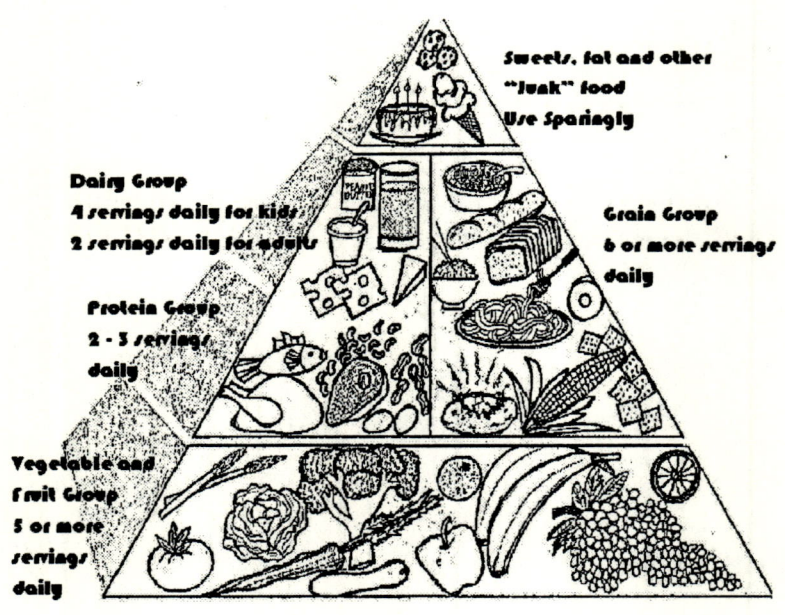

Figure 2 The Food Power Pyramid

By placing the fruits and vegetables at the base of your kid's diet, you are providing plenty of carbohydrates along with many of the vitamins, minerals and fibers that they need for health, growth and optimal performance.

Bunny Foxhoven, R.D.

Chapter 4

Energy Sources from Food

Food energy can be divided into three basic categories: Carbohydrates, proteins and fats. Much research has gone into finding out which foods our bodies prefer to use as fuel during exercise and activity. We know that at different intensity levels we use different amounts of fuels. During rest and low intensity activities such as slow walking or just moving around during the day, our bodies use about half carbohydrates and half fat as energy sources. As the intensity level, speed or demands of the activity increases, the body shifts towards using more carbohydrates and less fat for fuel. The protein requirement also appears to increase. However, not as quickly as carbohydrates. The following chart illustrates this.

Protein is represented in black, carbohydrate or glucose in gray, and fat in white.

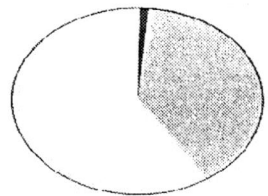

Rest
Protein (very little)
Carbohydrate/glucose (40%)
Fat (60%)

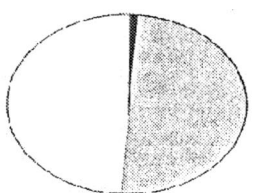

Mild intensity, long endurance exercise (about 50% Vo2 max or effort)
Protein (very little)
Carbohydrate/glucose (50%)
Fat (50%)

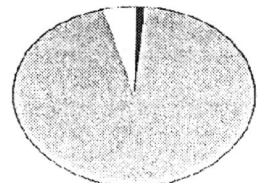

High intensity, short duration exercise (about 90%-95% vo2max)
Protein (very little)
Carbohydrate/glucose (95%)
Fat (5%)

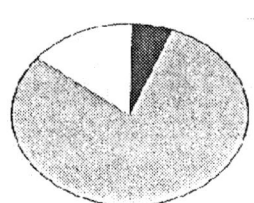

High intensity, long endurance exercise (about 70%-80% vo2 max)
Protein (5%-8%)
Carbohydrate/glucose (80%)
Fat (10%-15%)

Chart 1 Fuel source during exercise Source: Gatorade Sports Science Institute State of the Research Report 94.

This chart shows that carbohydrates are the preferred source of energy for exercise. During higher intensity workouts such as sprinting, lifting, pushing or any other short intense workout, the body burns a higher percentage of carbohydrate than fat or protein as fuel. At lower intensities, the body is able to convert some stored fat and protein into carbohydrates for fuel.

Carbohydrates come in many forms and perform various other functions in the body. Along with being the primary source of fuel for working muscles, carbohydrates are the only fuel our brains can use.

Bunny Foxhoven, R.D.

For quick energy, the body stores carbohydrates in three readily available energy forms; muscle glycogen, blood glucose, and triglycerides.

1. ***Muscle Glycogen*** - The muscles and liver can store a limited amount of glycogen that is readily available for energy. Glycogen is used during high intensity, short bursts of energy when very little oxygen is available. Activities like sprinting, power lifting and jumping rely on muscle glycogen. When using muscle glycogen, waste products such as lactic acid builds up in the muscles and rapidly leads to fatigue. This is why these high intensity activities can only be carried on for 15 to 30 seconds. Training can help improve the muscles ability to regenerate muscle glycogen and clear out the waste products so the athlete can continue playing at higher intensity levels. This is helpful in sports such as soccer, basketball, mountain biking and others where the athlete has both high and low intensity periods.

2. ***Blood Glucose*** - When carbohydrates are eaten prior to exercise, they are digested and broken down into smaller molecules that float around in the blood, called blood glucose or blood sugar. This blood glucose is readily available energy for the working muscles and other organs. The body must maintain a normal amount of blood glucose or sugar at all times because it is the only fuel that can be used by the brain. If the blood glucose level drops too low, the brain starves and can go into a coma. The body carefully maintains normal blood glucose levels by storing and removing sugar in different forms continually. If too much sugar or carbohydrates are eaten and the muscles don't require any more blood glucose at the time, the excess blood glucose is converted into fat and stored!

3. ***Triglycerides*** - A readily available form of blood glucose energy that can be stored as fat or broken down and used by working muscles as glycogen. Triglycerides are

primarily broken down and used for energy during lower intensity exercises such as jogging, walking or leisurely cycling. They are also used during rest and recovery to replace the used muscle glycogen and blood glucose.

Our bodies also have the ability to create carbohydrates out of protein or fat if there is not enough carbohydrate in the diet. However, high protein, high fat, low carbohydrate diets are not recommended for athletes because the protein and fat take too long to break down and turn into carbohydrates for fuel. Also, such a diet creates excess waste products that must be filtered out through the kidneys.

Although research on carbohydrate loading and pre-competition meals in children has not been done, some data suggests that young athletes will benefit from eating a diet similar to adult athletes. However, the food choices, timing and amount eaten should be supervised to ensure that the child is eating and drinking properly for the amount of training he or she is doing. Carbohydrates should be at least 55% and as high as 70% of the athletes total calorie intake. This is especially important for athletes in high-endurance sports or who are undergoing heavy training schedules. Chapter 12 will help you calculate how much carbohydrates your young athlete should be eating.

Research done on athletes playing in high intensity sports such as soccer, and basketball, show that when the athletes eat enough carbohydrates and eat them at the right times, their performance and endurance improved as much as 40% over athletes who did not eat enough carbohydrates! (1,5) Endurance cyclists, runners, and swimmers also perform longer and better when their diets include adequate amounts of carbohydrates.

Bunny Foxhoven, R.D.

Chapter 5

Carbohydrates

Carbohydrates are probably the most hotly debated and confusing nutrition topic of our time. Most weight loss programs and diet books focus on cutting down or eliminating carbohydrates, stating that "carbs can make you fat". Yet overwhelming research shows that they are extremely important in the athletes diet. When athletes don't get enough carbohydrates in their diet, performance decreases.

Carbohydrates are a complex subject in themselves. Some are great food choices and others have no nutritional value. Some are good for pre-game meals and others are better for after games. Carbohydrates come in many different forms and are found in almost every food. They can be classified as either sugars (simple carbohydrates), starches (complex carbohydrates) or fiber. Both sugars and starches contain 4 calories per gram, fiber contains no calories since our bodies cannot digest them.

Simple Sugars

I like to think of sugar molecules as links in a chain. Scientists symbolize simple sugar molecules by using an individual hexagon shape.

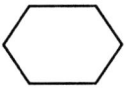

There are three different single sugar molecules called monosaccharides found in nature, that can be combined in a variety of ways to create longer chains called starches and fibers. These three monosaccharides combine to create foods with different flavors, sweetness' and tastes. All sugars are the final digestion product of tiny single or double chain molecules that the body uses for fuel. (6)

Monosaccharides

The three main single-molecule sugars, (also called monosaccharides) are:

Glucose
Fructose
Galactose

The body is able to use any of these sugars for energy. When sugar or starch foods are eaten, the body produces a chemical called "Insulin". If you are exercising or moving around and burning energy, the insulin transports the sugar into the working muscles and the body can burn it up as fuel. If you are not exercising and the muscles do not require any fuel, the insulin converts the sugar into a storable form called "fat." When you eventually need the extra calories, the fat is pulled back out of fat storage, broken back down into sugars, and burned up in the muscles as fuel.

Glucose is the end product of starch digestion. When "starchy" or "grain foods" such as wheat, bread, pasta, cereals and crackers are eaten, they are digested and broken down into smaller and smaller molecules. Eventually they are broken into individual glucose molecules which can be used by the muscles for energy. Glucose is also the main sugar in potatoes, rice, corn, and many other grains. All carbohydrate foods contain some amount of glucose, some contain a high percentage of glucose and some are very low.

Fructose is the main type of sugar found in fruits and vegetables and requires a little extra digestion time. Fruit is therefore, a good choice for meals and snacks when eaten at least one hour before exercise. Fruit can also be eaten during exercise if the intensity is low, such as walking or slow cycling. Fructose is found in all fruits and vegetables along with smaller amounts of glucose. It is also the sweetest of all of the sugars so less fructose is needed to sweeten the foods. It may cause stomach cramps, bloating and other digestive problems if too much is used at once, especially right before practice or games.

Galactose is found only in milk and milk products. It is less sweet than the other sugars which is why milk has only a mild sweetness. Galactose combines with Glucose in milk to form Lactose, the common name for milk sugar. Many people lack the enzyme "lactase" to break the lactose into its galactose and glucose molecules so they can not digest this milk sugar. Gas, bloating and discomfort as the galactose ferments in the stomach then occurs.

Even though fructose and galactose are slightly different molecules that require different enzymes to digest and use them efficiently, they are great sources of energy and should be included in the diet when possible.

Disaccharides

Disaccharides look like this: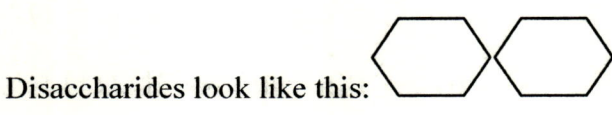

Sugars are more commonly found in foods as double chains called disaccharides The most common disaccharides are:

Lactose (milk sugar) - glucose and galactose combined
Sucrose (table sugar) - glucose and fructose combined
High fructose corn syrup (syrup for sweetening foods such as soda pop and candy) - glucose and fructose combined.
Honey - glucose and fructose with other flavoring, coloring molecules

All disaccharides must break down into single molecules before they are able to enter the blood stream and be used. This is not difficult for your body to do as the digestion process begins on the tongue! Just put a pinch of white table sugar on the tongue and watch what happens!

Most food contains sugar in some form and usually has combinations of these different sugars. The food manufacturers are required to list the total amount of all sugars that are in the product so that you are aware of what your child is eating. Read the ingredient list to be sure what the sugar sources are! A little sugar is OK, but be sure to see how much is in the foods you are buying and be aware of the times your child is choosing to eat them. Chapter 14 discusses the best times and food choices for your child before, during and after exercise.

Complex Carbohydrates

For more efficient storage of energy, plants and animals store these mono saccharide and disaccharides in long chains called complex carbohydrates. Plants pack carbohydrate energy into units called "starches" and animals and humans store carbohydrates in the muscle and liver in units called "glycogen." These longer chains of

Bunny Foxhoven, R.D.

sugars can contain several hundred simple sugars and are thus called "complex carbohydrates." Starches are found in all plants such as grains (wheat, oats and barley...) potatoes, rice, corn, vegetables and fruits.

Starch molecules are symbolized like this:

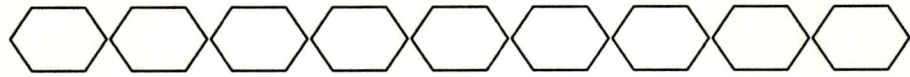

Humans and animals have digestive enzymes to break these starches into sugars for energy. The longer the chain, the longer it takes to break the starch into sugar. This is important to know when planning your child's pre-game or pre practice meals and snacks. If it takes too long to digest the food, it will still be in the stomach and intestines at game time resulting in problems such as bloating, gas, nausea and inability to continue playing. If the food is too simple or sugary and the digestion is too quick, the insulin may clear too much of the sugar out of the blood stream and into fat storage. Your child will then have too-low blood sugar and no energy by game time. This experience is called "a blood sugar crash" or hypoglycemia. Much research is going on concerning the effect starches have on exercise, blood sugar levels, energy production and athletic performance. Refer to chapter 14 for timing of meals and snacks.

Sports beverage and food companies use different combinations of these sugars and more complex starches to create great-tasting, fast-acting energy foods and drinks for athletes. Some work very quickly and contain higher amounts of sugars, and some work slower and contain more complex forms of carbohydrates. Some even contain more protein and fat for even slower digestion and absorption. Be sure to experiment with the different energy bars and drinks to find the ones that your child prefers and which ones work best in the given amount of time before practice and games.

Many of these energy bars and drinks also contain other chemicals and herbal additives such as caffeine, ginko biloba, guarana, or ephedra. Read the labels of the products that your children are choosing to be sure they are not getting unnecessary and/or unwanted additives in their foods!

Carbohydrates are extremely important for recovery after practice and games as well. As your child practices or works out daily, he or she uses up the stored muscle glycogen and must replace it before the next workout or game. (7,8) Research suggests that the first 1 - 2 hours after practice and games are the most important time to refuel the exhausted muscles. The graph below shows how the muscles begin to replace the used muscle glycogen when carbohydrates are included in the diet. Eating a diet rich in good sources of carbohydrates will completely restore muscle glycogen levels back to normal in 45 hours. In contrast, a low carbohydrate, high fat and high protein diets fail to replace the missing glycogen and will eventually lead to fatigue and inability to compete regularly.

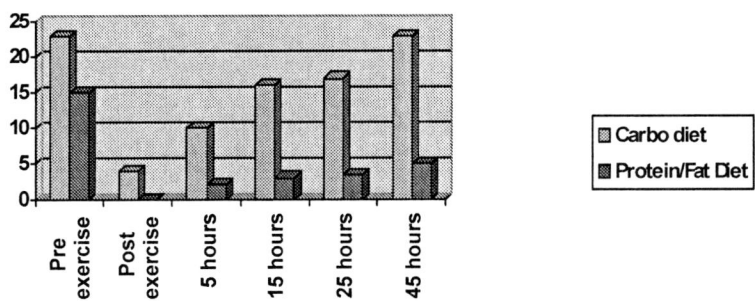

Chart 2 Muscle glycogen recovery time with/without carbohydrates.

Recent research has also shown that eating carbohydrates, along with a small amount of lean protein, will help replace the used muscle glycogen and repair and rebuild the muscle tissues most efficiently. (9)

Bunny Foxhoven, R.D.

fiber

Fiber is the most complex of all of the carbohydrates—so complex in fact that it is indigestible by humans! This is very important to human health for several reasons including heart health, energy metabolism, proper elimination, and water absorption. Fibers are classified into two groups.

Soluble fibers are the softer fibers found in beans, legumes, pectins, fruits, vegetables and some grains, such as oats, rice and corn. They have been found to help reduce blood cholesterol levels, thus protect against heart disease.

Insoluble fibers are the more "crude" or rough fibers contained in wheat and other grains. These fibers act more like a broom and clean out the intestinal tract as they pass through. Much research is continuing concerning the connection between insoluble fiber and cancer prevention.

Both types of fiber are necessary for good health and performance. Teach your young athletes to eat a well-balanced diet of both soluble and insoluble fibers for optimal health and performance. Use the following formula to calculate your childs daily fiber needs. Total daily fiber = "age (in years) + 5 to 10 grams per day" I.e. a 10 year old would need 10 + 5 to 10 grams = 15 - 20 grams of fiber per day. (10) Adults and fully grown children need 25 - 35 grams of fiber per day. It is not known if children have differing fiber needs than adults; however, a well-balanced diet that includes plenty of fresh fruits, vegetables and whole grains will ensure that children are getting plenty of fiber.

Table 2 below shows the common fiber content of many popular foods.

food	gm. fiber/serving	food	gm. fiber/serving
Cereals			
All Bran Cereal	10	Corn Flakes	1/2
Bran Flakes Cereal	5	Granola	5
Shredded Wheat Cereal	5	Raisin Bran Cereal	5
Corn Bran Cereal	5	Corn or Rice Chex	0
Fruit and Fibre Cereal	6	Oatmeal, instant pkt.	1 - 2
Total Cereal	3	Oatmeal, regular	4
Cheerios	3	Sugary kids cereal	0
Bran Chex	5		
Grain Products			
Bagel, white	<1	Bulgur	3
Bagel, Whole wheat	2 - 4	Barley	3
White bread	<1	Brown Rice	2
Whole wheat bread	2 - 4	White Rice	<1
Multi-grain bread	1 - 2	Pasta, regular	2
Corn tortilla	1	Pasta, whole wheat	2
Wheat tortilla	1 - 2	Bran muffin	3 - 6
Legumes			
Beans	5 - 7	Refried Beans	6
Food	**Gm. Fiber/serving**	**Food**	**Gm. Fiber/serving**
Legumes (cont.)			
Lentils	4	Dried peas	3 - 4
Vegetables			
Broccoli	3	Brussels sprouts	4
Carrots	2 - 3	Cauliflower	2
Corn	4	Spinach/greens	2 - 4
Potato	3	Tomato	2
Fruit			
Apple	2 - 3	Banana	2
Kiwi	3	Melons	2
Orange	3	Pear	4.5
Prunes	3	Berries	2 - 4

Information for this chart taken directly from food labels on market aisles.

Bunny Foxhoven, R.D.

Chapter 6
Glycemic Index

Nutrition professionals have discovered that various foods effect the blood sugar in very different ways. Some are digested quickly and turn into blood sugar quickly. Others are processed much slower. Scientists have created a formula to help determine how quickly a food is processed into useable energy. This formula is called this the "glycemic response". A foods glycemic response is determined by many factors such as the amount of simple sugars vs. starch in the meal, the amount of fiber, the volume eaten at one time, the amount of fat and protein in the food, and it's preparation. Researchers have created a way to help people determine when and how much of a food to eat based on its glycemic response by ranking them in the "glycemic index" chart. Foods with a high glycemic response have a value above 60, moderate foods fall between 40 to 60, and low fall below 40. When foods with high glycemic response are eaten along with those with a lower glycemic response, the digestion is significantly slowed down, thus the glycemic response is much lower. Table 3 shows the glycemic index of many popular foods. (11)

Glycemic index (GI) of many foods

Food	GI	Food	GI
High GI			
Pure Glucose	100	Sports Drinks	90 - 91
Instant Rice	91	Inst. mashed potato	83
Baked Potato	83	Microwaved potato	82
Corn Flakes	84	Hard candy	84

Rice Krispies	82	Rice Cakes	82
Grape Nut Flakes	80	Jelly/Gummy candy	80
Soda Crackers	79	Waffle	77
Doughnut	76	Wafer cookies	77
Corn Flakes	77	Cheerios	74
Oatmeal, inst. sugar	75	Inst. Cream of Wheat	74
Graham Cracker	74	Pure honey	73
Watermelon	72	Carrots	71
White bread	70 - 72	Whole wheat bread	65 - 75
Shredded Wheat	69	Soda Pop	68
Grape Nuts	67	Whole wheat cracker	67
Reg. Cream of Wheat	66	Couscous	66
Pineapple	66	White table sugar	65
Life Cereal	66	Raisins	64
Oatmeal, reg w/ sugar	65		
Ice cream	61 (ranges from 42 - 75)		

Moderate

Bran Muffin	60	Bran chex	58
Orange Juice	57	Boiled potato	56
Long cooking white rice	56	Brown rice	55
Popcorn, Plain	55	Corn on the cob	55
Oatmeal cookie	55	Potato Chips	54
Sweet potato	54	Cake	54 - 60
Banana	52	Chocolate	49
Green peas	48	Banana Bread	48
Bulgar	48	Baked beans	48
Lentil Soup	44	Orange	42
Oatmeal, long cook, plain	42	All Bran Cereal	42
Pasta noodles	41	Pumpernickel bread	41
Apple juice	41		

Low

Apple	36	Pear	36
Powerbar	30 - 35	Chocolate milk	34
Low fat flavored yogurt	33	Garbanzo beans	33
PR Bar	33	Lima Beans	32
Skim Milk	32	Dried Fruits	30 - 35

Lentils	29	Kidney Beans	27
Whole Milk	27	Barley	25
Grapefruit	25	Fructose	23
Soy Beans	18	Peanuts	14

Meats, Eggs and other pure proteins are less than 20!

Table 3

According to research done on athletes, the glycemic index of foods has a large impact on exercise and performance. Low and moderate glycemic index foods should be eaten 1.5 to 2 hours prior to exercise to provide sustained energy over the duration of the workout. High Glycemic index foods are so quickly digested that they are best used during and after exercise for muscle glycogen replacement. (11)

Chapter 7

Best Carbohydrate choices

Carbohydrates are also loaded with vitamins and minerals if they are not too highly processed or refined. See chapter 14 for ideas on pre-game and post-game meals, but the following foods are considered good daily carbohydrate choices. If your favorites are not listed here, that doesn't mean they are not good choices. I may have simply overlooked them so research them and find out if they are good sources of some vitamin, mineral or fiber! If the answer is yes, then your favorite food is probably a good choice also!

Vegetables are all great sources of carbohydrate! Some are higher in starch such as potatoes, corn and squash while others are loaded with fiber like Brussels sprouts, spinach and cabbage. Try to get your child to eat a wide variety of vegetables to get all of the vitamins and minerals found in this group. When shopping look for those that are the deepest color and that look and feel the freshest. Those that top the nutrition lists are: (12)

Red peppers	Carrots	Romaine Lettuce
Spinach	Green Peppers	Parsley
Broccoli	Green Peas	Endive
Tomatoes	Avocado	Bibb Lettuce
Cauliflower	Green Beans	Celery
Cabbage	Onion	Garlic

Fruits are important because they supply the body with many vitamins, minerals and fiber as well as providing an excellent source of carbohydrate for energy. Again look for those that are the best-colored and appear the freshest. All fruits offer some benefit,. Just try getting a variety into your child for optimal health. Some good ideas are:

Apples	Apricots	Bananas	Blueberries
Cantaloupe	Cherries	Dates	Figs
Grapefruit	Grapes	Honeydew	Kiwi
Mango	Orange	Peach	Papaya
Pear	Pineapple	Plum	Prunes
Raisins	Strawberries	Watermelon	

Cereals should be made with 100% whole grains. They may have a small amount of sugar added but any cereal with over 10 grams of sugar per serving is considered too sugary to be very healthy. Many cereals contain dried fruits such as raisins and dates, and this will raise the sugar content listed on the label. These cereals are fine unless they are also frosted! Some of the best cereal choices in my opinion are:

All Bran	Basic 4
Bran Buds	Bran flakes
Cheerios	Corn Bran
Corn Flakes	Crispie Wheats and Raisins
Fruit and Fibre	Grape Nuts/Flakes
Healthy Choice (all)	Life
Muselix	Nutrigrain
Oatmeal	Product 19
Quaker toasted oatmeal squares	Quaker Low fat Granola
Raisin Bran	Shredded Wheat/frosted or plain
Smart Start	Special K
Total	Wheaties
Wheat Chex	Wheatina
Wheat or Bran Chex	

Breads should be 100% whole grain. Many wheat breads are just white breads with carmel coloring and placed in a nice brown bag!

Read the label and make sure that there is whole grain flour as either the first or second ingredient. Breads have to have some white flour in them in order to rise, but they should have at least 2 grams of fiber per serving to be healthy. The more fiber the better!

Others

Bagels, preferably should be whole grain or contain 2 or more grams of fiber.
Pretzels
Graham Crackers
Low fat or fat free tortillas
Pasta
Rice, preferably long cooking or brown rice
Couscous
Crackers
Low fat cookies and granola bars

Bunny Foxhoven, R.D.

Chapter 8
Protein and Amino Acids

Protein provides the structure for all of our muscles, organs, blood and tissues. Every child needs to get protein in their daily diet to ensure that the body has all of the building blocks necessary for daily repair and growth. Proteins are made up of smaller particles called "Amino Acids". There are 21 different amino acids found in foods. Nine of these amino acids are called essential amino acids, which means that we must get them from the foods we eat. (only eight of the amino acids are essential to adults because we develop the ability to create histidine as we mature.) The remaining 12 amino acids can be synthesized in the body from other amino acids.

The following chart outlines the essential and non-essential amino acids:

Essential amino acids for children

Histidine	Isoleucine	Lysine	Leucine
Methionine	Phenylalanine	Tryptophan	Valine

Non-Essential amino acids for children

Alanine	Asparganine	Aspartic Acid	Arginine
Cysteine	Cystine	Glutamic Acid	Glutamine
Glycine	Proline	Serine	Tyramine

Chart 3 Essential amino acids

Animal proteins, such as meat, eggs and dairy products, contain all nine of the essential amino acids we need to survive. Vegetables and grains contain varying amounts and different combinations of the essential amino acids but are always lacking a few. The human body is able to put the amino acids together in various combinations, like a building block set, to create complete proteins as it needs them.

Vegetarians need to eat a wide variety of grains, legumes and vegetables to ensure that they are getting all the protein they need. A good way to do this is called "combining proteins." Eating foods together from different food groups such as peanut butter on whole grain bread, beans on a tortilla, or vegetables and rice together will provide all of the essential amino acids needed for your body to build proteins.

Many people have a hard time getting enough protein. Others eat way too much. If you don't eat enough proteins, your body will not have all of the building blocks necessary for tissue repair, blood cell development, immunity, energy use and most importantly for optimal growth! For adults, the protein needs are defined by the amount needed to repair and rebuild tissues. Children have the additional needs for growth. During rapid growth spurts children are at their highest protein requirement.

Recent research has shown that athletes need slightly more protein than non-athletes. (13) This is due to increased repair and rebuilding of muscle tissue. Protein also has an important role in providing fuel for aerobic exercise.

For adults, the requirements are .8 to 1 gram of protein per kilogram of body weight per day (approximately .37 to .5 grams of protein per pound of body weight.) Growing kids need slightly higher amounts of protein. The National Research Council in 1998 reported that kids aged 7 - 10 need 1.1 - 1.2 grams per kilogram per day and 11 - 14 year olds need approximately 1 gram per kilogram per day. (14) (To calculate weight in kilograms, divide your weight in pounds by 2.2)

Bunny Foxhoven, R.D.

Protein must be eaten in sufficient amounts daily to provide for all of the building, rebuilding and repair of tissue. The following chart will help you determine the amount of protein your child needs daily. (gram ranges = 1.0 to 1.2 gm/kg body weight for different ages)

Amount of protein needed per day in grams and ounces		
Weight in pounds	Grams of Protein/day	Ounces of Protein/day
40 - 50	18 - 27	2 - 2.5
50 - 60	23 - 33	2.5 - 3
60 - 70	27 - 38	3 - 3.5
70 - 80	32 - 43	3.5 - 4
80 - 90	36 - 49	4 - 4.5
90 - 100	41 - 54	4.5 - 5
100 - 110	45 - 60	5 - 5.5
110 - 120	50 - 65	5.5 - 6
120 - 130	54 - 71	6 - 6.5
130 - 140	59 - 76	6.5 - 7
140 - 150	64 - 81	7 - 7.5
150 - 160	68 - 87	7.5 - 8
160 - 170	73 - 93	8 - 8.5
170 - 180	77 - 98	8.5 - 9
180 - 190	82 - 103	9 - 9.5
190 - 200	87 - 109	9.5 - 10
200 - 210	91 - 114	10 - 10.5

Chart 4 grams of protein needed daily based on body weight.

It is recommended that children younger than ten years have the following amounts of protein: (15)

Age	grams protein/kg body wt/day
0 - 6 months	2.2
6 months - 1 year	2.0
1 - 3 years	1.8
3 - 6 years	1.5
7 - 10 years	1.2

This may sound like a lot of protein needed every day until you turn it into servings of foods. It turns out that children get sufficient amounts of protein from drinking a few glasses of milk and eating 1 - 2 slices of meat per day! Most children will eat something with protein without too much argument.

If you worry that your child doesn't eat enough protein, try adding cheese, cottage cheese, thin sliced meat, tuna or eggs to a salad. Encourage them to snack on fruits along with some peanut butter or nuts. Or try adding milk, yogurt, peanut butter, soy milk or protein powder to a fresh fruit smoothie. Many energy bars and sports drinks include good amounts of protein as well. It really isn't difficult to get enough protein. However, I do run across athletes that focus so much on low-fat, vegetarian diets that they neglect their protein needs and end up weak, anemic, injured and constantly sick.

This chart below illustrates the average amounts of protein in common foods:

Food	Amount	Grams of protein
Tuna, white fish, turkey, egg white	3 oz.	28 – 30
95% lean beef, chicken, game meat	3 oz.	24 – 28
90% lean beef, dark fish, dark meat chicken/turkey	3 oz.	20 – 25
80% - 90% lean beef, lamb, veal, organ meat	3 oz.	17 – 22
Cottage cheese	4 oz ½ cup	13 – 20
Milk	8 oz.	8 – 10
Tofu	½ cup	7 – 8
Beans, lentils, peas	½ cup	7 – 9
Seeds	1 oz	6 – 9
Nuts	1 oz	6 – 8
Vegetables	1 cup	2 – 4
Fruit	1 piece	0

Chart 5 Grams of protein in foods. (taken from averages from food labels)

Note that some foods have more calories than others based on their fat content. eg: nuts have the same amounts of protein as meat per ounce, but more calories! Protein, like carbohydrates, contains 4 calories per gram. If you eat a food that contains protein, you multiply the grams of protein by 4 to get the calories from protein in that food, eg. tuna with 30 grams of protein would supply 120 protein calories. Most foods are a combination of protein, carbohydrates and fat. You would be better off looking at the total grams of protein your child is eating rather than concerning yourself with percentages and calories!

Chapter 9

Best Protein Choices

The best protein choices are those that are high quality, low in fat, don't contain preservatives or additives, and taste good! Kids have very different tastes. Most kids don't like very strong tastes or unique textures, but some kids love them. Below is a list of the most common healthy protein foods that kids like.

Be aware Meats (should contain no more than 10% fat by weight)

Chicken: Baked breast, thigh or leg; roasted-sliced lunch meat, ground chicken breast.

Turkey: Baked breast thigh or let, roasted-sliced lunch meat, ground turkey, lean turkey sausage or pepperoni, lean turkey bacon.

Fish: Any cooked fresh fish, canned tuna or salmon.

Beef: 90% lean or greater ground beef, roast beef, lean steaks such as flank, ribeye, tenderloin, eye of the round, rump or filet.

Pork: Lean cuts such as tenderloin, rump roast, ham, or lean chops.

Eggs: Scrambled, boiled or cooked in pan with oil spray.

Beans: Kidney, great northern, pinto, low fat refried beans, or any others in this family of beans.

Bunny Foxhoven, R.D.

Nuts: Almonds, cashews, peanuts, peanut butter, pecans, walnuts and others.

Soy: Soy beans, edamame, tofu, soy milk, tempeh, miso.

TVP: Textured Vegetable Proteins make up a large portion of the vegetarian offerings such as veggie patties, veggie dogs and breakfast links.

Chapter 10

Fat

Dietary fat is a complex subject. Eat too much, and you suffer the consequences—weight gain, heart disease, cancer, and other health risks. Don't eat enough, you also suffer hunger, boredom with food and, possible nutrient deficiencies. The answer then lies in finding both the right amount to eat for a young growing body and the right types of fat to eat for a healthy heart and body. The American Heart Association and the American Dietetic Association say that the average American eats too much fat, (approximately 40% of our calories come from fat) and that we eat too much of the bad types of fat. They recommend that we start limiting the amounts of fat in foods, particularly "Junk foods", down to around 25 to 30% of our total calorie intake. This is particularly important for children as National statistics are showing that children are eating more and more high fat, high sugar, low nutritional value foods. AND children are getting heavier and heavier at younger ages. To help your child avoid these problems be sure to provide wholesome meals that provide a good balance of carbohydrates, protein and fats.

Basically, there are three types of fat; Saturated, Monounsaturated and Polyunsaturated fat.

Saturated fats are hard at room temperature such as lard, bacon grease or shortening. Our bodies need saturated fat to create cholesterol, a white waxy fat found naturally in your body that is used in the development of the nervous system and for building cell walls. After the first two years of life, very little saturated fat is needed to maintain the nervous system. Research has shown that people who eat too much saturated fat have higher cholesterol levels and are at higher risk for heart disease. Although it is not known how much saturated fat is too much for children, it is a good idea to start teaching your children now and avoid health problems in the future.

Monounsaturated fats are primarily found in olive, peanut and canola oils. The research done to date shows that these fats have heart-protective properties and that people who choose more monounsaturated fats than the other types of fat have lower risk of heart disease and some forms of cancer!

Polyunsaturated oils come mostly from vegetable sources. They are highest in corn oil, safflower oil and sunflower oil. These fats do not appear to be bad for your heart, but they don't seem to be as good at protecting your health as the monounsaturated fats. The current recommendation is that around 30% of your child's **total calories** should come from fat and that 1/3 should be from saturated fat, 1/3 from monounsaturated fat and 1/3 from polyunsaturated fat.

Percentages of Fat

This chart shows the percentage of saturated, monounsaturated, and polyunsaturated fats in common fats found in foods.

Type	% Saturated	% Mono	% Poly
Canola	6	62	32
Olive	14	77	9
Peanut	18	49	33
Safflower	10	13	77
Sunflower	11	20	69
Corn	13	25	62
Soybean	15	24	61
Cottonseed	27	19	54

Margarine	17	24	34
Chicken Fat	31	47	22
Lard	41	47	12
Beef Fat	52	44	4
Palm Kernel Oil	81	11	2
Coconut Oil	92	6	2

Table 4 Types of fat. Source: Composition of Foods, U.S. Dept. of Agriculture (15)

*Important tip to remember! All fat has 9 calories per gram, and about 130 calories per tablespoon. No matter how saturated it is, too much fat can still be fattening!

If your child is underweight and needs more calories, it is acceptable to add more good fats to the diet. If he or she is overweight, it may also be acceptable to limit some of the fat in his or her diet. In most cases, children who are overweight are simply eating more than 30% of their calories as fat anyway, and limiting them to 30% is a healthy alternative to dieting!

Chapter 12 shows you how to figure out how many total calories and fat grams your child should be eating daily. Use these calculations and charts above to determine the proper amount for your child.

Lowering Saturated Fats in the Diet

Some recommendations for lowering the saturated fat and cholesterol in your child's diet are:

1. Cut down on high-fat meats such as sausages, bacon and high fat ground meats, such as 70% lean hamburger.
2. Read food labels to be aware of hidden fats, especially palm kernel and coconut oils since they may have "no

cholesterol" posted on the front of the package yet are high in saturated fat!
3. Remove the skin and visible fat from poultry and all meats.
4. Try more vegetarian meals that contain protein from beans, soy, nuts or vegetables.
5. Switch to low-fat or naturally fat-free snacks such as fruit, pretzels, fig cookies or granola bars in place of candy, cookies, pastries or chips.
6. Switch to skim and low-fat dairy products.

The following are some label reading tips to help you understand the information printed on the labels about fat and cholesterol. (16)

- **Fat free** - must have less than .5 grams of fat per serving.
- **Light** - has at least 1/3 less fat than the original product or a similar regular fat product.
- **Low fat** - contains three or less grams of fat per serving.
- **Low saturated fat** - has less than one gram of saturated fat per serving.
- **Lean** - must contain less than 10 grams of total fat and less than 4 grams of saturated fat.
- **Extra lean** - means less than 5 grams of total fat and 2 grams of saturated fat.
- **Cholesterol free** - has less than 2 grams of cholesterol per serving.
- **Low cholesterol** - contains less than 20 milligrams of cholesterol per serving.
- **Reduced** - must contain at least 25 % less fat than the original product or a similar regular fat product.

Be sure to flip the package over and read the nutrition label for actual totals of fat, saturated fat and cholesterol because some foods are tricky. Remember that vegetable products won't naturally contain any cholesterol so don't be fooled into thinking that "cholesterol free" also means "fat free" by the front of the package!

Fat-soluble vitamins are very important for health. Much research is continuing concerning the amounts children and adults need for health and longevity. Vitamins A, D, E and K are fat soluble vitamins, and the best sources are vegetable oils, almonds, peanuts, sunflower oil, safflower oil and sesame seeds, whole grains and wheat germ. Other foods, such as fish oil, fish, eggs, dairy products and fortified foods, are also good sources of these fat soluble vitamins.

A final thing to remember is that fat takes a long time to digest—approximately 3 to 5 hours. So be aware of the amount of fat in the foods you are feeding your children right before practice or games as it will still be bouncing around in their stomach causing nausea and cramping if eaten too close to the event. See the chapter on timing of foods for more specific information.

Bunny Foxhoven, R.D.

Chapter 11

CHOLESTEROL

Contrary to popular belief, cholesterol is not a fat even though it is often associated with fat. It is however, a wax like substance that is made in your liver from fat. Cholesterol does have a few important purposes. It coats and insulates each nerve fiber in our nervous system, which makes it especially important in the first 2 years of a child's life as the nervous system is developing. It is also used in the creation of fat-digesting enzymes. Too much, however, and it begins to build up in our blood. As it flows through our arteries, it can begin to get clogged in the arteries and start to form a plaque. This eventually leads to hardened and narrowed arteries and eventual heart attack.

The level of blood cholesterol that is considered "safe" is 200mg/dl, but you are still considered at risk for having a heart attack if your level of good cholesterol is too low or bad cholesterol is too high. Doctors use a "risk ratio" to determine if your cholesterol levels are within an acceptable range rather than looking solely at your total cholesterol level. There are several different forms of cholesterol (also called lipoproteins) Some are good and some are bad. Some people are lucky enough to have a liver that produces very little cholesterol. The cholesterol that it does make is mostly the top quality, high density lipoproteins (hdl's) type of cholesterol. Other less fortunate people have a liver that likes to make mostly low-density lipoproteins (ldl's), and make a lot of it! Fortunately this can be changed, if even a little, through diet and exercise!

It is not known how important cholesterol levels are in growing children.

Most doctors do not even look at the numbers until the child is fully grown. However, if there is heart disease in the child's family, it might be smart to start the child eating a heart-healthy diet and develop good habits early!

If you are worried about your children's cholesterol or ldl levels:

1. Limit the amount of saturated fats they eat (remember the kind that are turned into cholesterol!) to less than 10% of their total calorie intake or 1/3 of their fat intake.
2. Increase the fats coming from vegetable oils, especially from olive, avocado, nut, and canola oils.

This "heart smart" diet is a good idea for everyone, not just those who have already had a heart attack. Reduce your risk of heart attack and get in shape all at once!

Bunny Foxhoven, R.D.

Chapter 12

Calculating your child's calorie needs

The most important thing to remember when planning your children's meals is that their hunger level is going to vary every day! Some days they are going to be famished and eat everything in sight, other days you may feel that they are going to starve themselves! These fluxuations are considered normal, and you should not worry about them if they don't go on for too long. Usually if children are allowed to decide how much they want to eat, they will make a good choice. Be sure to keep an eye on their intake, however, because overeating and eating disorders are a growing concern in our society.

Calculating the calorie needs of a young athlete is difficult and varies during growth spurts and high activity days. The World Health Organization created the following chart based on childhood averages of weight, height and activity levels. (17,18,19). If your child is above or below average in any of these areas, remember to increase or decrease these numbers, or they will not be accurate!

Begin by Calculating your child's average daily calorie needs (DCN) from the chart below.

Average Daily Resting and Activity Calorie Needs

(calories are based on average growth and activity levels, they do not include sports training calories)

Age In Years	Males Resting cal. Needs	Ave. Activity Needs	Females Resting cal. Needs	Ave Activity Needs
3 - 9	22.7 X BW	495	22.5 X BW	499
10 - 17	17.5 X BW	651	12.2 X BW	746
18 +	15.3 X BW	679	8.7 X BW	496

*BW = Body Weight in Pounds

Chart 6 Average daily calories needs.

Step one: Find your child's age in years.

Step two: Go across the table to factor for resting calorie needs for males or females.

Step three: Multiply that factor by your child's body weight in pounds. This equals the amount of calories your child needs just to rest all day (breathe, digest, heart beat, think).

Step four: Add "average calorie needs for activity" for your child's age and sex. If your child is very active or seems to have boundless energy and can't seem to get enough to eat, add more calories for daily activity, he or she has a higher metabolism. If he or she is the opposite, subtract a few calories, he or she may not need as many calories.

Step five: add step three and four together. This equals the amount of calories your child burns in an average day (DCN) **But**

Bunny Foxhoven, R.D.

Remember this does NOT include calories used in practice or games! Step six will show you how to add calories used in exercise.

OPTIONAL METHOD

You can use he following chart if you want a simpler way to find calories your child needs daily. These are JUST averages of all children and do not account for your child being above or below average for height, weight or activity. I have included this chart if you want to skip all of the above calculations and just use an average!

Calorie Needs of average children

Age	Calorie Needs/day
0 - 5 months	650
6 - 12 months	850
1 - 3 years	1300
4 - 6 years	1800
7 - 10 years	2000
11 - 14 year old boys	2500
11 - 14 year old girls	2200
15 - 18 year old boys	3000
15 - 18 year old girls	2200

Chart 7 (taken from oxygen media, 1998)

For athletic children, you need to add the calories that they burn up during practice and games in addition to their daily calorie needs. To calculate these additional calories, use the "Exercise and Activities" chart below.

Bunny Foxhoven, R.D.

Exercise and Activities Chart

Calories used per hour
Exercise per lb. of body weight

Exercise	Calories
Super high intensity exercise group Aerobics - high intensity, Elliptical training, Handball, Martial arts, Rock Climbing, Running (8 min mile pace),	4.6 - 6.5
High intensity exercise group Circuit training, Cycling (15 + mph), Cross Country Skiing, In line Skating, Jumping Rope, Rowing (boat or machine), Running (10 min mile pace), Ski Machine, Stair Climb Machine	4.0 - 4.5
Moderate High Intensity Group Aerobics - low intensity, Basketball, Cycling (12 mph), Football, Hockey, Ice Skating, Racquetball, Snow Shoeing, Soccer, Swimming Freestyle, Tennis Singles, Weight Training	3.0 - 3.9
Moderate Intensity Exercise Group Baseball, Cycling, (10 mph), Softball, Dancing (social), Downhill Skiing, Golf (carrying clubs), Hiking, Kayaking, Skate Boarding, Walking (hills, 17 min mile pace), Water Skiing, Wrestling	2.0 - 2.9
Low Intensity Exercise Group Cycling (6 mph), Dancing (slow), Golf (not carrying clubs), Horseback Riding, Surfing, Ultimate Frisbee, Volleyball, Walking (flat, 17mm), Yoga	1.0 - 1.9

*These numbers are based on averages for people of all weights and heights and did not include children in their research. It is only assumed that children burn calories similarly to adults.

Chart 8 Exercise calories. Information compiled from references 7, 20, 21,

Step six: Find your child's sport or activity in the chart above.

Step seven: Multiply your child's body weight by the number of calories used per hour per pound of body weight found in that sport. (be sure to account for times when your child exercises longer than one hour.) This equals the additional calories your child uses for sports training and games.

Child's body weight in pounds (_____)X Calories used per hour per pound of body weight (_____) = Calories used by child in one hour of specific activity, or "exercise calories" (EC)

For example: a child that plays tennis for 2 1/5 hours per day and weighs 78 pounds would need:

78 pounds X 3.0 - 3.9 = 235 to 304 calories per hour

Since he plays for 2.5 hours, 235 to 304 X 2.5 = 587 to 760 additional calories for the 2 ½ hours of exercise!

Step eight: Add daily calories needs (DCN) step five + Exercise Calories (EC) step seven. This equals the calories your child needs to eat daily for optimal health, growth and exercise.

NOW that you know how many calories your child should be eating AND since no one likes to have to count calories (especially children), the following chart is a simple breakdown of calories. It will show you how many servings from each food group your child should eat to get all of the required calories.

Bunny Foxhoven, R.D.

Calories	Protein Ounces	Dairy 1 cup	Fruits 1 serving	Veggies 1 serving	Grains 1 oz.	Grams of fat 30% of total
1800	6	3	3	3	9	60
1900	6	3	3	3	10	63
2000	7	3	3	3	10	66
2100	7	3	3	3	11	70
2200	8	3	3	3	11	73
2300	8	3	3	3	12	76
2400	8	3	3	3	13	79
2500	8	3	4	3	14	83
2600	9	3	4	3	14	86
2700	9	3	4	3	15	89
2800	9	4	4	4	15	93
2900	10	4	4	4	15	96
3000	10	4	4	4	16	99

Chart 9. Calories and estimated servings per day. These numbers are approximations based on average portions.

Chapter 13

Vitamins And Minerals

Originally the words "vitamins" and "minerals" referred to the micronutrients **in foods** that kept us healthy and energetic. With the onset of the industrial world, advertising and changes in American eating habits, these words more than likely bring to mind compact little pills we call supplements. The vitamin and mineral supplement industry has become a multi billion dollar industry due to so many of us using them as insurance against disease and in place of good eating habits.

Scientists have discovered many chemicals in foods that may contribute to better health, vitamins, minerals, electrolytes, phytochemicals, phytoestrogens, and others. Many of their functions are well known and documented while others are not yet fully understood. We do know, however, that cultures with people who eat diets rich in fruits, vegetables and whole grains have lower incidence of disease than people with poor nutritional habits.

Vitamins are metabolic catalysts or chemicals in foods that regulate the biochemical reactions in your body. In other words, they make things happen correctly in your body. Scientists have discovered 13 vitamins to date and have determined each one's specific function in the body. The Food and Nutrition Board and the National Academy of Sciences created the US Recommended Dietary Allowances (RDA's) to help us determine if the foods we eat are providing all of the 13 vitamins we need daily. Those 13 vitamins, their function and best sources are listed in chart # 10 below.

Bunny Foxhoven, R.D.

Vitamin	Function	Best Food Source	Age/Sex	RDA
A retinal	Antioxidant protects eyes, skin, digestive & respiratory tracts Deficiency = night blindness	Dark leafy greens and bright orange/red veggies and fruits eg.: carrots, apricots, red peppers, pumpkin, spinach, broccoli…	0 – 1 1 - 3 4 - 6 7 - 10 M 11 + F 11 +	375 RE 400 RE 500 RE 700 RE 1000 RE 800 RE
D chole-calciferol	With calcium and phosphorus metabolism for bones and teeth	Dairy products, fortified grain products, must be activated in skin by sunlight!	0 - 6 mo MF 1 - 24 Adults	7.5 mcg 10 mcg 5 mcg
E tocopherol	Antioxidant protects skin & cell walls	Oils, nuts, wheat germ, whole grains, green leafy veggies	0- 6 mo 6 mo - 1 1 - 3 4 - 10 M 11 + F 11 +	3 TE 4 TE 6 TE 10 TE 10 TE 8 TE

K	Necessary for proper blood clotting	Dark green leafy veggies, broccoli, kale	0 – 6 mo 6 mo - 1 1 - 3 4 - 6 7 - 10 M 11 - 14 M 15 - 18 M 19 - 24 M adults F 11 - 14 F 15 - 18 F 19 - 24 F adult	5 mcg 10 mcg 15 mcg 20 mcg 30 mcg 45 mcg 65 mcg 70 mcg 80 mcg 45 mcg 55 mcg 60 mcg 65 mcg
C Ascorbic Acid	Antioxidant necessary for healthy skin, connective tissue, bone, teeth and cartilage, and enhances immune system	Citrus fruits, tomatoes, peppers, potatoes, berries, melons, broccoli, fortified drinks, juices	0 – 6 mo 6 mo - 1 1 - 3 4 - 10 11 - 14 15 + Safe limit	30 mg 35 mg 40 mg 45 mg 50 mg 60 mg 500 mg
B 1 Thiamin	Helps metabolism turn carbohydrates into energy	Whole grains, fish, lean meats, most fresh fruits and veggies	0 - 6 mo 6 mo - 1 1 - 3 4 - 6 7 - 10 M 11 - 14 M 15 + F 11 +	.3 mg .4 mg .7 mg .9 mg 1 mg 1.3 mg 1.5 mg 1.1 mg

B 2 Ribo-flavin	Used in metabolism for energy release, healthy skin, respir-atory and digestive tracts and nervous system	Fresh fruits and vegetables, whole grains, red meats, dairy products	0 - 6 mo 6 mo - 1 1 -3 4 - 6 7 - 10 M 11 - 14 M 15 - 18 M 19 + F 11 +	.4 mg .5 mg .8 mg 1.1 mg 1.2 mg 1.5 mg 1.8 mg 1.7 mg 1.3 mg
B 3 Niacin	Necessary for converting food into energy, growth and production of hormones	Fish, potatoes, red meat, nuts, mushrooms, whole grain cereals, starchy vegetables	0 - 6 mo 6 mo - 1 1 - 3 4 - 6 M 7 - 10 M 11 - 14 M 15 - 18 M 19 + F 11 +	5 NE 6 NE 9 NE 12 NE 13 NE 17 NE 20 NE 19 NE 15
B 5 Panto-thenic acid	Used in the metabolism of carbs, fat and protein	Eggs, nuts, whole grains, wheat germ, meat, fish, green veggies	0 - 6 mo 6 mo - 3 4 - 6 7 - 10 11-adults	2 mg 3 mg 4 mg 5 mg 7 mg
B 6 Pyridoxin	Necessary in the creation and breakdown of amino acids and in metabolism	Meat, poultry, fish, beans, eggs, nuts, spinach, bananas, fortified cereals	0 - 6 mo 6 mo - 1 1 - 3 4 - 6 7 - 10 M 11 - 14 M 15 + F 11 - 14 F 15 - 18 F 19 +	.3 mg .6 mg 1 mg 1.1 mg 1.4 mg 1.7 mg 2 mg 1.4 mg 1.5 mg 1.6 mg

Folate	Used in the production of blood cells and for the nervous system	Fresh fruits and veggies, especially green leafy and citrus, beans and peas	0 - 6 mo 6 mo - 1 1 - 3 4 - 6 7 - 10 M 11 - 14 M 15 + F 11 - 14 F 15 +	25 mcg 35 mcg 50 mcg 75 mcg 100 mcg 150 mcg 200 mcg 150 mcg 180 mcg
B 12 Cyano- cobal-amine	Needed for the metabolism of food, production of red and white blood cells, and strengthens memory	Meat, poultry, eggs and dairy	0 - 6 mo 6 mo - 1 1 - 3 4 - 6 7 - 10 11 +	.3 mcg .5 mcg .7 mcg 1 mcg 1.4 mcg 2 mcg
Calcium	Formation of bones, teeth. Also in nerve and muscle function and kidney filtering, creation of enzymes	Dairy products, fortified juices, canned fish, fortified cereals, spinach	0 - 6 mo 6 mo - 1 1 - 10 11 - 24 25 +	400 mg 600 mg 800 mg 1200 mg 800 mg
Phos-phorus	Formation of bones, teeth, part of dna/rna & used in energy metabolism	Meat, fish, poultry, dairy, eggs, bread, legumes and nuts	0 - 6 mo 6mo - 1 1 - 10 11 - 24 25 +	300 mg 500 mg 800 mg 1200 mg 800 mg

Mineral	Function	Sources	Age	RDA
Mag-nesium	Used w/ calcium for bones, protein synthesis, part of energy enzymes, nerve & muscle function	Legumes, nuts, whole grains, green leafy veggies	0 - 6 mo 6 mo - 1 1 - 3 4 - 6 7 - 10 M 11 - 14 M 15 - 18 M 19 + F 11 - 14 F 15 - 18 F 19 +	40 mg 60 mg 80 mg 120 mg 170 mg 270 mg 400 mg 350 mg 280 mg 300 mg 280 mg
Iron	Heme iron for the transport of oxygen and carbon dioxide on red blood cells, enzyme production	Red meat, poultry, fish, fortified grains, small amounts in some fruits and veggies	0 - 6 mo 6 mo - 10 M 11 - 18 M 19 + F 11 - 50	6 mg 10 mg 12 mg 10 mg 15 mg
Zinc	Cofactor for enzymes, growth, healing, taste, insulin function, immunity	Meat, liver, eggs, seafood, dairy products, whole grains, legumes	0 - 1 1 - 10 M 11 + F 11 +	5 mg 10 mg 15 mg 12 mg
Potas-sium	Fluid-electrolyte balance, nerve & muscle function	Meat, milk, vegetables and fruit	All ages	2000 - 5500 mg = safe

Chart 10. Vitamin and mineral RDAs. Source: Food and Nutrition Board, National Academy of Sciences, RDA' revised 1989

Athletes may have slightly higher metabolic needs for some nutrients such as calcium, b vitamins and iron. However, since athletes usually eat larger amounts of food than non-athletes, their vitamin and mineral intake is usually larger as well.

A further discussion of some of the more noteworthy vitamins and minerals follows:

Calcium - Growing children need calcium for bones, teeth and nervous system development. Adults need calcium for maintaining them. Exercise has been shown to increase bone density and help prevent osteoporosis. Yet, calcium must be present in the athletes diet to provide the building blocks for those growing bones and nerves. The best sources of calcium are dairy products, fish (with the bones still in such as sardines), green leafy veggies and calcium fortified foods and juices. Growing children need 800 to 1200 mg of calcium per day (see chart above).

Iron - Iron is necessary for carrying oxygen to working muscles and carrying carbon dioxide waste products away from the muscles. A deficiency of iron is called "anemia" and results in fatigue, being "out of breath", and decreased performance in athletics. Iron is most prevalent in meat products, yet iron fortified foods (cereals, crackers, breads, and others) are common and general well liked by kids.

B Vitamins - The B vitamins (thiamin, riboflavin, niacin, folic acid, B6/pyridoxin and B12/cyanocobalamine) are often called "the energy vitamins". This is because they are highly involved in the metabolism of food and production of muscle energy. Fortunately B vitamins are found in many places; fruits, vegetables, whole grains and fresh meat and dairy products. The fresher, less-processed foods are better sources of the B vitamins.

Antioxidants - The major antioxidants are Vitamin A, Vitamin C and Vitamin E. There are many other smaller "micronutrients" that are also wonderful antioxidants. Scientists are learning more and more every day about the "health protective" properties of these antioxidants. We know that they may help protect us against cancer, heart disease and strokes. Athletes may need more antioxidants than non-athletes due to the increased demands for oxygen during practice and games.

Many people still like to take a multivitamin/mineral supplement for insurance. Just to make sure that they get everything they need daily. This is OK as long as you are not giving your children "mega doses" of anything and that you don't spend a fortune to get it. Most over the counter multi vitamins are good quality and give the extra boost kids need. Check the label to be sure they don't supply more than 100 or 200 % of the RDA for any of the above listed substances.

One final note on vitamins and minerals— Foods contain dozens of other nutrients called micronutrients that are important to your health and vitality. When you eat a well-balanced diet that contains plenty of fresh fruits, veggies, whole grains and lean meats and dairy products, you will be eating all of these micronutrients along with the other important nutrients listed above. Most of these micronutrients are thought to help prevent cancer, heart disease and other life threatening diseases!

Part two

Nutrition for Sports Performance

This section contains information on the best food choices for breakfasts, lunches, dinners and snacks as well as information on the best timing for these meals for optimal performance. You should have your children fill out the "Food Preference Survey" at the end of this book and then go over these lists with them to get an idea of what their food preferences are. This will help you plan your meals accordingly. You can also use these lists to simply check the appropriate boxes when shopping!

You and your child should begin experimenting right away with the right foods, timing of meals and snacks and recovery foods to determine what is best for him or her! Don't wait until the day before a big game or tournament to try something new. Listen to your children and teach them to listen to their body. Every one is different so what works for you may not work best for them.

Bunny Foxhoven, R.D.

A Parent's Guide to Sports Nutrition for Young Athletes

Table of Contents

Chapter 14 63

Timing of meals and snacks

Chapter 15 66

Breakfast

Chapter 16 70

Lunch

Chapter 17 73

Dinner

Chapter 18 75

Snacks

Chapter 19 81

Food Preference Survey for Traveling Teams

Bunny Foxhoven, R.D.

Chapter 14
Timing of meals and snacks

The *ideal timing of meals and snacks* are listed below each title (eg., Basic Breakfasts, Lunches, Dinners, and Snacks). This is very important because you must allow for certain digestion times prior to activity. Also, post game meal timing is important to replenish the used energy stores and aid in muscle recovery.

If your children are in a tournament in which they play multiple games or have more than one competition in a day and may not have time to eat regular meals, the timing of the food intake becomes even more important. Every situation is different in terms of game times, so here are *some general guidelines* to help you choose meals and snacks that fit your game schedules.

- Pre-game meals should be eaten at least 1.5 - 4 hours prior to start of warm-up time.
- A pre-game meal that is eaten 2 - 4 hours prior to game time can include foods which have higher protein content. These foods are listed as "Additional Foods" under the breakfast, lunch, dinner or snack categories in the following chapters.
- Post-game meals should be eaten as soon as possible following the end of game, preferably within one hour.

- If a post-game meal won't be eaten within 1 hour following the game, a snack should be eaten (for example, if the game ends at 9:30 a.m., eat a snack after the game and them eat a normal lunch). For suggested snacks, see "Snacks" in chapter 18.
- For multiple same-day games, meals or snacks eaten between games should be dictated by the timing of the next game to be played. If you only have 1 - 2 hours prior to the next game time, the athlete should choose foods from the "Snacks" list. The snacks should be eaten soon after the finish of the game to allow for digestion.
- These same suggestions apply even if there are 3 or more games in a day.
- The meal eaten on the night before a game should contain primarily complex carbohydrate, along with some protein, such as chicken, turkey, or fish and a large serving of veggies.
- Be cautious with sugary foods, including sports drinks and energy bars. Some athletes experience a drop in blood sugar (due to insulin reacting to the sugar) which causes them to feel tired, sluggish or light headed. Your child can learn how to listen to their body's signals and eat appropriately to control their energy levels during practices and games.
- Allow adequate time for food to digest. All athletes are different, so have them begin now, during practice, experimenting with which foods and times work best with their digestive tract and metabolism.
- Experiment with liquid meals (fruit smoothie or blended breakfast cereal shake) if your child has a "finicky" stomach and can tolerate liquids better than solids.
- Occasionally some athletes simply get too jittery and cannot tolerate foods in the early morning. In this case, an extra-large bedtime snack may help

them stay more nourished in the morning. Be aware that carbohydrates digest better than protein or fats while sleeping, so choose foods from the snack lists that are primarily carbohydrate or ones that contain only a small amount of protein and are easily digested, i.e.: a bowl of cereal, a peanut butter and jelly sandwich or even just a piece of fruit.

Bunny Foxhoven, R.D.

Chapter 15

Breakfast

You've heard it thousands of times, "Breakfast is the most important meal of the day." That's because it is! By putting a good, nutritious breakfast in your child, you are preparing him or her for the day. Breakfast provides the calories, vitamins, minerals and all of the things your child needs for learning, growth and exercise. Research has shown numerous times that children who eat healthy breakfast learn better in school, stay more focused and have more energy for sports. If your child skips any meal it should NOT be breakfast.

Many children complain that they are not very hungry in the morning. This could be due to eating too much in the evening before they go to bed. If this is the case, have them trim back on the amount they are snacking on in the evening. Alternatively, have them switch to lower fat items such as fruit, cereal or pretzels instead of chips, ice cream or cheeses. By cutting down on the amount they eat, they should wake up hungrier and be able to put something in their stomach.

If your child has an early morning workout and cannot eat before a morning workout, at least try to get him or her to eat or drink something light. Some diluted fruit juice, a sports drink, an energy bar or a piece of fruit will give him or her the energy to practice harder and more efficiently. After practice make sure he or she has a good supply of foods to eat to replenish and recover for the day. This is particularly important if the child has another practice or workout scheduled for that day or if he or she is going on to school and needs the energy to learn! If he or she just **cannot** eat anything before working out, have them eat a substantial snack before bed. After practice a good, well- balanced breakfast is very important.

Some kids don't like typical breakfast foods. There's no rule saying that they need to eat cereal, waffles or eggs every day! Have them try things like leftover pizza, Chinese food or chicken and mashed potatoes! There are some very healthy, quick options at the market nowadays. Have a few of these around:

Lean pockets
Frozen breakfast burritos
Egg and ham English muffins
Chicken quesadillas
Cottage cheese and fruit cup
Yogurt with granola
Cheese and crackers
Peanut butter and crackers
Tortilla wraps
A sandwich

To make breakfast time less stressful, make extra leftovers of your child's favorite dinner foods and freeze them in individual baggies for a quick warm up for breakfast. This will make your morning smoother and there will always be something to eat, even if your morning routine is hectic and short of time.

Breakfast should consist primarily of wholesome carbohydrates along with a small amount of lean protein and fat. The following are great breakfast ideas for both pre and post workout days.

Bunny Foxhoven, R.D.

Basic Breakfasts

Pre-game meals should be eaten 1.5 to 4 hours prior to the start of the warm up time before games. Below is a list of good healthy breakfast choices. If breakfast is eaten more than 4 hours prior to game time, the athlete should have an additional snack in between breakfast and game time (see snack list).

- Cold Cereal

Wheaties	Total
Raisin Bran	Bran Flakes
Mini-Wheats	Toasted Oatmeal
Muslix	Basic 4
Oatmeal Squares	Wheat or Bran Chex
Cheerios	Others listed in Chapter 9

- Hot cereal, such as oatmeal or cream of wheat, with a small amount of sugar or honey added. The pre-flavored packages have 6 to 9 teaspoons of sugar!
- Skim, 1% or 2% milk
- Soy milk, calcium fortified (may also use rice milk for allergies)
- Low fat yogurt, variety of flavors
- Fruit Smoothies made with fresh fruit, yogurt and ice
- Whole grain bagels or English muffins (whole wheat, oat bran or multi grain)
- Low-fat, whole grain fruit muffins or bran muffins (NO pastries)
- Bread and toast (100% whole wheat or Iron Kids white)
- Jam, low fat cream cheese and butter
- Peanut butter, 1 - 1 1/2 tablespoons only
- Fresh fruit plate. These fruits are best for pre-game meals: apples, pears, bananas, berries, oranges, kiwi, peaches, nectarines and grapefruit (save other fruits for post-game meals and snacks)
- Fresh juices: orange, apple, grape, grapefruit

Additional Breakfast Items

If you will be having breakfast greater than 2 hours prior to game time, these items can be added along with the Basic Breakfast items

- Scrambled eggs or omelet without meat or cheese (vegetables are okay)
- Pancakes (oat bran pancakes are best, see recipes section)
- French toast made with whole wheat bread
- Whole grain waffles (Nutrigrain or Whole grain Eggos)
- Syrup, jam or applesauce (Go light on syrup to avoid feeling sluggish during game).
- Cottage cheese
- Hot cocoa or cold chocolate milk
- Low fat sweet bread such as Banana or zucchini bread

Breakfast Items containing protein

If you have more than 3 hours prior to the game to eat, you may add these foods your breakfast menu:

- Low fat Canadian bacon or turkey bacon
- Omelets with cheese, Canadian bacon and/or veggies
- English muffin pizzas (made with Canadian bacon or turkey bacon and part skim mozzarella cheese)
- Deli meat sandwich on whole grain bread
- Whole grain bagel sandwich
- Low fat lunchmeat such as turkey, chicken, boiled ham or tuna
- Hash brown potatoes made with very little oil
- Nuts and dried fruit trail mix
- Protein powder that can be added to smoothies
  EAS Advant-Edge
  Carnation Instant Breakfast
  Myoplex
  Genisoy
  Pure Pro

Bunny Foxhoven, R.D.

Chapter 16

Lunch

The following foods are good choices for lunch. They should be eaten at least 1.5 to 2 hours before starting warmups for your game. If there is not at least 1.5 hours before game time to eat lunch, the athletes should choose foods from the snack list and eat a larger lunch after the game. If lunch is eaten more than 4 hours prior to game time, the athlete should have an additional snack in between lunch and game time (see snack list).

- Fresh fruit plate or fruit salad (Apples, pears, oranges, grapefruit, bananas, peaches, nectarines and berries.)

- Small assortment of vegetables (Carrots, cucumbers and tomatoes, no hot or spicy vegetables)

Sandwiches (choose either deli tray items or pre-made sandwiches)

Pre-made Sandwiches
- Bagel sandwich with lean deli meat
- Tortilla wraps with lean deli meat
- Tortilla wraps with sliced chicken breast
- Deli sandwich on whole grain bread

Deli Tray Sandwich Items:
Assortment of breads
- Whole wheat
- Iron Kids white

- Pita bread
- Whole grain bagels
- Sub rolls
- Tortillas

Variety of Lunchmeats or spreads
- Turkey
- Tuna
- Chicken
- Ham
- Peanut butter

Condiments
- Mustard
- Low fat mayonnaise
- low fat salad dressing
- catsup

Broth Based Soups (low fat, if possible)
- Chicken, turkey noodle, or rice
- Minestrone
- Bean soup with a broth base, not a thickened bean base

Additional Lunch Items

The following items can be added to the basic lunch menu above IF the meal is eaten 2 hours or more prior to game time:

Side Dishes
- Cottage cheese
- Low fat pasta salad
- Cole slaw
- Rice pilaf
- Macaroni salad

Low fat Carbohydrate Dishes
- Spaghetti with marinara sauce

Bunny Foxhoven, R.D.

- ❑ Baked potato with small amount of butter, cheese or low fat sour cream
- ❑ Rice pilaf or herb rice dishes (no fat)
- ❑ Chicken and rice or pasta
- ❑ Low fat refried or black bean burrito

Fresh Steamed Vegetables
- ❑ Carrots
- ❑ Green beans
- ❑ Broccoli
- ❑ Mixed vegetables

Desserts
- ❑ Fruit Newton cookies
- ❑ Graham crackers / animal crackers
- ❑ Strawberry shortcake
- ❑ Angel food cake with berries
- ❑ Low fat granola bars
- ❑ Health Valley cereal bars
- ❑ Fresh fruits
- ❑ Low fat pudding

Chapter 17

Dinner

These foods are good choices for post game meals and meals eaten on the night before games. If chosen as a post game meal, they should be eaten within 1 hour after the game. If you know that it will be longer than 1 hour prior to eating a post game meal, it would be beneficial to have a small snack that includes both carbs and protein available for the athletes to eat within 30 minutes post game (see snack list).

Main Dishes

- Spaghetti with meatballs and sauce, a fresh salad.
- Pasta primavera with chicken or shrimp.
- Lasagna made with lean beef and low fat cheese.
- Pizza with Canadian bacon and vegetables (preferably not sausage or pepperoni).
- Pasta with marinara sauce, chicken and vegetables.
- Stir-fried beef or chicken with vegetables and rice or noodles.
- Baked chicken and baked potatoes with mixed vegetables.
- Chicken or beef fajitas.
- Lean beef such as sirloin tips, ribeye, or tenderloins with rice, potatoes or pasta and vegetables.
- Chicken or beef vegetable kabobs with potatoes and vegetables.
- Pasta and beans with vegetables.
- Stuffed shells with marinara sauce and vegetables.

Bunny Foxhoven, R.D.

- California style pizza (light on the cheese, more vegetables).
- Hamburger with lean beef or turkey burger, salad and baked potato.
- Burrito with low fat refried or black beans, chicken, or beef and vegetables
- Chili with cornbread or roll and vegetables.
- Sliced turkey or lean roast beef French dips with a salad or vegetables.
- Bagel sandwich with sliced deli meat and salad or vegetables.
- Pita sandwich with deli meat and vegetables.
- Sub sandwich with real meat (no luncheon meats).

Vegetables / Side Dishes

- Fresh salad with low fat dressing
- Cucumbers
- Tomatoes
- Steamed veggies such as carrots, broccoli, squash
- Rice pilaf
- Baked potatoes (Avoid French fries)
- Whole grain roll, tortilla, bread, crackers, or pretzels

Chapter 18

Snacks

Children have to snack. Their stomachs are not usually large enough to hold enough calories to make it to the next meal! It is much healthier for them to eat slightly smaller meals and have healthy snacks in between. Help them examine their daily routine and determine the best time and amounts for their meals and snacks. Many times we associate junk food with snack food. It is important that these snacks are not junk, they are needed for growth and energy and should provide your child with vitamins, minerals, fiber and energy. Foods that are primarily sugar and fat are fine to have in small amounts, possibly along with or after a healthier snack. Things like cookies, cakes, pastries and pies should take a back seat to fruits, nuts and dairy products. A list of the best snack choices and the optimal time to eat them has been included below.

Pre-Game Snacks

These are good choices for snacks *if there is only 1 hour between games*

- Fresh fruit: Apples, applesauce, pears, oranges, grapefruit, berries, bananas, apricots, peaches, nectarines.
- Pretzels
- Whole grain low fat crackers

- Whole grain, multi grain or oat-bran bagels
- Low fat whole grain or bran muffins
- Frozen fruit bar (Dole, Tropicana or Welch's real fruit juice bars)
- Small peanut butter and jelly sandwich

- Sports Bars (carbohydrate rich, such as:)
- Gatorbar
- Powerbar
- Powerbar Harvest
- Cliff Bar
- Luna Bar or Pria Bar for females
- Tiger's Milk Bar
- Peak Bar
- Low fat granola bars
- Carnation Breakfast Bar

Sports drinks are designed to re-fuel exercising muscles. They work best if consumed 10 - 15 minutes prior to warm up, throughout the game and for recovery after the game. Sports drinks may have an adverse effect on blood sugar levels if they are consumed too long before game time. It is best not to drink them from 20 to 60 min prior to game time. SODA IS NEVER A GOOD OPTION. They are too high in sugar and can cause dehydration. Many people find that slightly diluting a sports drink helps with absorption and flavor! EXPERIMENT and see which works best.

Sports Drinks Like Gatorade will actually help your child stay hydrated better as they contain small amounts of electrolytes that help your body absorb the water. They also taste better, and many athletes find that they drink more if they like the flavor!

Additional Snack Items

These snacks can be added to the list above for snacks that are eaten 1.5 hours or more prior to game time.

- Low fat muffins
- Graham crackers
- Dry cereal (Honey Nut Cheerios, Quaker Oat Squares, Honey Nut Shredded Wheat, Cheerios, Low fat Granola, Raisin Squares)
- Sweet breads (banana bread, zucchini bread, etc.)
- Dried fruit (small amounts)
- Yogurt
- Raw veggies
- Rice cakes with jam or peanut butter
- Peanut butter and jelly sandwich on whole grain bread or Iron Kids white
- Baked corn or potato chips
- Fruit smoothies

Bunny Foxhoven, R.D.

Post Games Snacks

These snacks should be eaten soon after the end of a game if the team will not be eating a meal within 1 hour of the end of the game. A good ratio is 1 gram of protein to 4 grams of carbohydrates (read the label if your favorite snack is not listed below!)

- Post game fruits: Bananas, watermelons, cantaloupe, honeydew, grapes, plums, pineapple and other tropical fruit.
- Small meat or peanut butter sandwich
- Peanut Butter and low fat crackers
- Nuts and Dried fruit
- Yogurt
- Energy bars
    - PR bar
    - Balance bar
    - Powerbar Pure Pro
- Replacement Drinks
    - EAS Advant-edge
    - Carnation Instant Breakfast
    - Revenge
    - Accelerade
    - Scitrex the edge

Late Night Snacks

Many young athletes will need to eat another late night snack. The following snacks are good ideas to keep in their room for such occasions.

- Fresh fruit, any
- Quaker low fat chewy granola bars
- Nature Valley granola bars
- Nutrigrain cereal bars
- Kellogg's rice krispie treats
- Health valley pop tarts, cereal bars or breakfast pastries
- Nuts and dried fruit trail mix
- yogurt
- Low fat cheese and low fat crackers
- Dry cereal
- Milk
- Bagels
- Muffins

Bunny Foxhoven, R.D.

Foods and Drinks Athletes Should Try to Avoid

Regular or Diet Soda Pop
Alcohol
Hot Dogs
Luncheon Meats, i.e.: bologna, salami, pepperoni, etc
Fried Foods, i.e.: fried chicken fingers, fried cheese, French fries, donuts, etc
Fatty Meats, i.e. ribs, sausage, etc.
Pastries
Candy and Candy Bars
Greasy Fast Foods
Fried Chips
Highly sugared cereals

Chapter 19

Food Preference Survey for Traveling Teams

Name_____Age_____Team____
Phone#_____Alt.Phone#_____
Height_____Weight_____

Medical History (anything I may need to know about their health) i.e.: allergies, stomach aches…

_____
_____
_____
_____
_____

Typical daily food and fluid intake (list child's food choices they typically make) also note how many oz. water they drink daily

Breakfast

Snack

Lunch
Snack

Dinner

Bunny Foxhoven, R.D.

List your child's favorite foods or foods they prefer for games
___
___
___
___
___
___

List foods your child won't eat
___
___
___

Part Three

Recipes

The following pages contain healthy, fun and tasty recipes for the entire family. I have included only recipes what contain less than 30% fat, are high in fiber and are loaded with vitamins and minerals. All of the recipes have been taste tested on real kids and given "approval" by them for including in this book! I hope you enjoy!

Bunny Foxhoven, R.D.

A Parent's Guide to Sports Nutrition for Young Athletes

THE LIGHTER SIDE OF COOKING

THE RECIPES

Bunny Foxhoven, R.D.

A Parent's Guide to Sports Nutrition for Young Athletes

TABLE OF CONTENTS
RECIPES

Chapter 20 89

Beverages and Appetizers

Chapter 21 94

Soups On

Chapter 22 106

Sensational Salads

Chapter 23 118

Super Side Dishes

Chapter 24 128

In From the Orient

Chapter 25 137

A Taste of Italy

Chapter 26 157

South of the Border

Bunny Foxhoven, R.D.

Chapter 27 174

Down Home U.S.A

Chapter 28 190

Veggies and Then Some

Chapter 29 198

Best Bakery

Chapter 30 211

Sinless Desserts

Chapter 20

Beverages and Appetizers

1. Fresh Fruit Frosties
2. Fresh Fruit Smoothies
3. Impossible Eggnog
4. Sheepherders Spinach Dip

Bunny Foxhoven, R.D.

Fresh Fruit Frosties

Ingredients:

1 c. fresh fruit equivalent
1 c. skim milk or non fat yogurt for thick frostie
1 cup ice cubes

Directions:

Blend on high until smooth and creamy, serve. Makes 2 1 c. servings.

Nutrition Information:

Total calories	Total grams protein	Total grams carbohydrate	Total grams fat
121	5	25	0

Significant source of the following vitamins, minerals and other nutrients:

Vitamins A, C and D, Calcium and Potassium

Fresh Fruit Smoothies

Ingredients:

1 banana
1/2 cup non fat plain yogurt
12 oz. orange juice
1/2 cup ice

Directions:

Place all ingredients in blender and blend 1 minute. Makes 2 1 cup servings. Variation; use 1 peach, 1/2 cup strawberries or other berries in place of banana or pineapple juice in place of orange juice.

Nutrition Information:

Total calories	Total grams protein	Total grams carbohydrate	Total grams fat
310	12	51	1

Significant source of the following vitamins, minerals and other nutrients:

A, C, D, Calcium and Potassium

Bunny Foxhoven, R.D.

Impossible Eggnog

Ingredients:

1 cup skim milk
1 egg
1 t. vanilla extract
2 - 3 large ice cubes
4 t. sugar
nutmeg

Directions:

Place all ingredients except nutmeg in blender and blend until thick and foamy. Pour into cup and sprinkle with nutmeg. Makes 4 1/2 cup servings.

Nutrition Information:

Total calories	Total grams protein	Total grams carbohydrate	Total grams fat
66	5	1.5	5

Significant source of the following vitamins, minerals and other nutrients:

Calcium and Vitamin D

Sheepherders Spinach Dip

Ingredients:

10 oz. box frozen spinach
1 pkg dry vegetable soup mix (2 - 3 oz.)
5-6 scallions, chopped
1/2 c. light or nonfat sour cream
1/2 c. nonfat plain yogurt
1/2 c. 1 % cottage cheese
1 large loaf sheepherders or sourdough bread

Directions:

Thaw spinach and drain all juice, add all ingredients and stir until smooth and well mixed. chill. Cut off top of bread loaf, hollow out center and cut into chunks for dipping. Place chilled dip mix into center and serve cold.

Nutrition Information:

Total calories	Total grams protein	Total grams carbohydrate	Total grams fat
139	5	18	5

Significant source of the following vitamins, minerals and other nutrients:

Vitamin A, Vitamin C, Calcium, Thiamin Riboflavin, Niacin

Bunny Foxhoven, R.D.

Chapter 21

Soups On

1. Winter Vegetable Stew
2. Old Fashioned Beef Stew
3. Sausage Lentil Soup
4. Turkey Noodle Soup
5. Black Bean Soup
6. Pasta Fagiloi (Bean and Pasta Stew)
7. Minestrone
8. Tomato Rice Soup
9. 3 Alarm Chili
10. Tortilla Soup
11. Chili Non Carne

Winter Vegetable Stew

Ingredients:

1 large onion, diced	2 large carrots, sliced
2 stalks celery, sliced	1 turnip, chopped
2 leeks, chopped	4 small potatoes, cubed
16 oz. whole peeled tomatoes, chopped	1 c. frozen corn
1 c. frozen peas	1 c frozen cut green beans
1/2 t. marjoram	1/2 t. oregano
4 cubes beef bullion	2 quarts water

Directions:

Place all ingredients in large pot, bring to boil, reduce heat and simmer 1 or more hours. Serves 8 1 1/2 cup.

Nutrition Information:

Total calories	Total grams protein	Total grams carbohydrate	Total grams fat
134	4	26	1

Significant source of the following vitamins, minerals and other nutrients:

Vitamins A, C, Thiamin, Riboflavin, Niacin, Potassium, Iron, Lycopene and Phosphorus

Bunny Foxhoven, R.D.

Old Fashioned Beef Stew

Ingredients:

1 Lb. lean beef from sirloin, flank or roast, cubed
1 large onion, diced
2 large carrots, sliced
2 stalks celery, sliced
1 turnip, chopped
2 leeks, chopped
4 small potatoes, cubed
16 oz. whole peeled tomatoes, chopped
1 c. frozen corn
1 c. frozen peas
1 c frozen cut green beans
1/2 t. marjoram
1/2 t. oregano
4 cubes beef bullion
2 quarts water

Directions:

Place all ingredients in large pot, bring to boil, reduce heat and simmer 1 or more hours. Serves 8 1 1/2 cup.

Nutrition Information:

Total calories	Total grams protein	Total grams carbohydrate	Total grams fat
252	18	26	7

Significant source of the following vitamins, minerals and other nutrients:

Vitamins A, C, Thiamin, Riboflavin, Niacin, Potassium, Lycopene, Iron and Phosphorus

Sausage Lentil Soup

Ingredients:

1/2 cup dried lentils
3 cups water
2 beef bouillon cubes
1 medium onion, chopped
1 carrot, sliced
1 stalk celery, sliced
1 large potato, grated
4 oz turkey sausage (see recipe in this book)
1 bay leaf
1 t. vinegar
1/4 t. thyme
1/4 t. pepper
3 T. parsley

Directions:

Bring lentils, water and bouillon cubes to boil in large pan, remove from heat, cover and let stand 1 hour. Add remaining ingredients and simmer covered for 1 hour. Serve hot garnished with parsley. Serves 8.

Nutrition Information:

Total calories	Total grams protein	Total grams carbohydrate	Total grams fat
179	8	11	8

Significant source of the following vitamins, minerals and other nutrients:

Vitamin A, Potassium, Phosphorus, Iron and Fiber

Bunny Foxhoven, R.D.

Turkey Noodle Soup

Ingredients:

12 oz chopped turkey, light meat is leanest
16 oz. bag noodles, any shape
16 oz. bag frozen mixed vegetables, any variety you choose!
8 scallions, chopped
4 cups chicken bouillon
1/2 t. black pepper
1/4 t. celery salt

Directions:

Bring to boil 1 gallon water, toss in all other ingredient except noodles. cook on medium high for 1 hour. Pour in noodles and cook until noodles are soft, approximately 15 minutes. serve hot. Makes 12 servings.

Nutrition Information:

Total calories	Total grams protein	Total grams carbohydrate	Total grams fat
272	15	28	8

Significant source of the following vitamins, minerals and other nutrients:

Vitamins, A, C, Thiamin, Potassium, Phosphorus and Iron

Black Bean Soup

Ingredients:

1 cup dried black beans
8 cups water
3 bouillon cubes
2 bay leaves
1 onion
2 stalks celery
2 cloves garlic, minced
1 each: red, green and yellow bell pepper, chopped
1/2 t. crushed red pepper
1/2 t. basil
1 1/2 T. vinegar
1/2 cup plain nonfat yogurt
2 T. parsley

Directions:

Soak beans overnight to soften. Drain and place in large pot. Add water and bouillon cubes and boil for 2 1/2 hours. Add spices and vegetables to beans and cook 1/2 hour. Serve in bowls with spoon of yogurt and parsley sprinkled over top. Makes 6 cups.

Nutrition Information:

Total calories	Total grams protein	Total grams carbohydrate	Total grams fat
84	5	15	.5

Significant source of the following vitamins, minerals and other nutrients:

Vitamins A, C, Thiamin, Potassium, Phosphorus, Iron and Fiber

Bunny Foxhoven, R.D.

Pasta Fagiloi (Bean and Pasta Stew)

Ingredients:

1 medium onion, chopped
1 medium bell pepper, chopped
3 cloves garlic, minced
1 32 oz. can tomatoes, chopped
1 16 oz. can kidney beans
1 16 oz. can garbanzo beans
6 oz. package pasta shells, elbow, or other small noodle
1 c. water
1/2 t. oregano
1/4 t. basil
1/8 t. black pepper

Directions:

Using some liquid from tomatoes sauté onion, bell peppers and garlic until soft. Add tomatoes and beans, bring to a boil and add pasta and spices, reduce heat and simmer until pasta is tender. Continue to simmer until desired thickness is achieved. Sprinkle with parmesan cheese if desired. Serves 8.

Nutrition Information:

Total calories	Total grams protein	Total grams carbohydrate	Total grams fat
209	8	40	2.5

Significant source of the following vitamins, minerals and other nutrients:

Vitamin C, Thiamin, Niacin, Potassium, Calcium, Phosphorus, Lycopene and Iron

Minestrone

Ingredients:

4 cups water
4 cloves garlic, minced
1/4 t. black pepper
1 8 oz. can tomato sauce
1/3 c. cooking sherry
1 16 oz. can kidney beans with liquid
1 16 oz. can lima beans, with liquid
1 cup uncooked whole wheat macaroni noodles
1/4 c. parsley, chopped
2 celery stalks, chopped
1 large carrot, chopped
1 small onion, chopped
1/2 c. cabbage, chopped
2 small potatoes, chopped
1 cup zucchini, chopped
1/2 cup cut green beans

Directions:

Mash 1/2 of the kidney and lima beans, place in large pot, add all ingredients except noodles to pot, stir and bring to boil, cover and simmer 35 minutes. Add noodles and cook 20 minutes until noodles are soft. Serves 8

Nutrition Information:

Total calories	Total grams protein	Total grams carbohydrate	Total grams fat
218	10	60	1.5

Significant source of the following vitamins, minerals and other nutrients:

Bunny Foxhoven, R.D.

Vitamins A, C, Thiamin, Potassium, Phosphorus, Iron and Fiber

Tomato Rice Soup

Ingredients:

2 32 oz cans whole peeled tomatoes, plus juice
1/2 small chopped onion
1/4 t. cloves, ground
1/2 cup long grain brown rice, uncooked
1 cup peas
1 cup corn

Directions:

Combine tomato juice, onion, cloves and rice and bring to a boil. Add peas and corn and simmer 4 to 5 minutes until peas and corn are cooked through. makes 8 1 cup servings.

Nutrition Information:

Total calories	Total grams protein	Total grams carbohydrate	Total grams fat
124	4	25	1

Significant source of the following vitamins, minerals and other nutrients:

Vitamins A, C, Potassium, Iron and Leutine

3 Alarm Chili

Ingredients:

1 lb. lean ground beef or turkey
3 30 oz. cans chili beans in chili gravy (preferably hot)
1 16 oz can pork and beans
2 32 oz. can whole peeled tomatoes, chopped
2 T. ground red pepper
1 small onion, chopped
1/4 t. basil
1/4 t. oregano
1/4 t. cumin
1 t. or 2 cloves garlic, minced or

Directions:

Brown ground beef or turkey, drain off excess grease, add onion, garlic and other spices. add beans, peppers and tomatoes, simmer 1 or more hours. Makes 16 1 c. servings.

Nutrition Information:

Total calories	Total grams protein	Total grams carbohydrate	Total grams fat
342	24	37	9

Significant source of the following vitamins, minerals and other nutrients:

Vitamins A, C, Thiamin, Riboflavin, Niacin, Potassium, Iron, Leutine and Phosphorus

Bunny Foxhoven, R.D.

Tortilla Soup

Ingredients:

8 flour or corn tortillas, cut into strips
1 medium onion, chopped
2 cloves garlic, minced
1 28 oz, can whole peeled tomatoes
4 chicken bouillon cubes
4 cups water
1 cup fresh cilantro, chopped
1/2 t. pepper
4 oz. fat free cheddar cheese for topping

Directions:

Place all ingredients except tortillas and cheese in large pot. Bring to boil, reduce to simmer 5 minutes. Ladle 1 cup over tortilla strips placed in bowl. Top with 1/2 oz cheese. Serves 8.

Nutrition Information:

Total calories	Total grams protein	Total grams carbohydrate	Total grams fat
133	7	17	4

Significant source of the following vitamins, minerals and other nutrients:

Vitamin C, Thiamin, Potassium and Iron

Chili Non Carne

Ingredients:

1 c. chopped carrots
1 c. chopped zucchini
1/2 c. corn
3 30 oz. cans chili beans in chili gravy
1 16 oz. can pork and beans
2 32 oz. cans whole peeled tomatoes, chopped
1 small onion, chopped
1/4 t. basil
2 T. ground red pepper
1/4 t. oregano
1/4 t. cumin
1 t. or 2 cloves garlic, minced

Directions:

Combine all ingredients in large pot and simmer for 1 or more hours to desired thickness. Makes 16 1 c. servings.

Nutrition Information:

Total calories	Total grams protein	Total grams carbohydrate	Total grams fat
195	7	32	4

Significant source of the following vitamins, minerals and other nutrients:

Vitamins A, C, Thiamin, Riboflavin, Niacin, Potassium, Iron,, Leutine and Phosphorus

Bunny Foxhoven, R.D.

Chapter 22

Sensational Salads

1. Creamy French Dressing
2. Russian Salad Dressing
3. Fruity Fresh Fruit Salad Dressing
4. Spinach Salad
5. Mandarin Orange Vegetable Salad
6. Pasta Salad
7. Pasta Salad Primavera
8. Pasta Crab Salad
9. Oriental Chicken Salad
10. Taco Salad

Creamy French Dressing

Ingredients:

2 T. lemon juice
2 T. wine vinegar
1/2 t. paprika
1/2 t. dry mustard or 1 t. prepared mustard and decrease vinegar to 1 T.
1/8 t. pepper
1/8 t. tarragon
3/4 c. plain nonfat yogurt.

Directions:

Combine in container with tight fitting lid, shake well and chill. Makes 8 servings.

Nutrition Information:

Total calories	Total grams protein	Total grams carbohydrate	Total grams fat
15	1	1.5	.5

Significant source of the following vitamins, minerals and other nutrients:

Calcium and Vitamin C

Bunny Foxhoven, R.D.

Russian Salad Dressing

Ingredients:

3/4 c. cider vinegar
3/4 c. water
2 T. lemon Juice
1 T. onion, chopped
1 T. dry mustard or 2 T. prepared mustard and less vinegar
1 t. garlic powder
1/8 t. pepper
1/2 t. paprika

Directions:

Combine all ingredients in container with tight fitting lid. Shake well and chill. Makes 10 servings.

Nutrition Information:

Total calories   Total grams protein   Total grams carbohydrate   Total grams fat
2   0   0   0

Significant source of the following vitamins, minerals and other nutrients:

Not a significant source of nutrients

Fruity Fresh Fruit Salad Dressing

Ingredients:

3/4 cups fruit flavored nonfat yogurt, any flavor
1/4 c. orange juice
1/8 t. ground cinnamon
1/8 t. nutmeg
1/4 t. grated orange rind

Directions:

Combine all ingredients in bowl, mix lightly and chill. Covers fruit salad for 4 - 6.

Nutrition Information:

Total calories	Total grams protein	Total grams carbohydrate	Total grams fat
34	1	7	0

Significant source of the following vitamins, minerals and other nutrients:

Calcium and Vitamin C

Bunny Foxhoven, R.D.

Spinach Salad

Ingredients:

Salad
8 cups fresh spinach
2 cups bean sprouts
2 cups fresh mushrooms, sliced
4 hard cooked eggs, sliced
1/3 cup Canadian bacon, cooked and diced
4 green onions, sliced

Sweet and Sour Dressing

1/2 t. sugar
1 T. catsup
1 T. vinegar
1/2 t. Worcestershire sauce
pinch salt and pepper

or

Sesame Dressing

1 T. lemon juice
1 t. soy sauce
1 T. toasted sesame seeds
1 t. honey
1/2 garlic clove, minced
pinch salt and pepper

Directions:

Wash and tear spinach into bite sized pieces, add remaining ingredients and toss with either dressing. Refrigerate and serve cold. Makes 8 1 cup salads.

Nutrition Information:

Total calories	Total grams protein	Total grams carbohydrate	Total grams fat
98	11	10	2

Significant source of the following vitamins, minerals and other nutrients:

Vitamins A, C, Thiamin, Riboflavin, Niacin, Potassium, Iron,, Leutine and Phosphorus

Bunny Foxhoven, R.D.

Mandarin Orange Vegetable Salad

Ingredients:

2 10 1/2 oz. cans mandarin orange segments, drained
2 cups cauliflower, chopped
1/3 c. green pepper, chopped
2 c. fresh spinach leaves, chopped
1/4 c. vinegar
1 T. lemon juice
1/4 t. onion powder
1/4 t. oregano

Directions:

Prepare and toss all ingredients in large salad bowl. Serve chilled. Makes 4 1 c. servings.

Nutrition Information:

Total calories	Total grams protein	Total grams carbohydrate	Total grams fat
77	3	16	.5

Significant source of the following vitamins, minerals and other nutrients:

Vitamins A, C, Thiamin, Riboflavin, Niacin, Potassium, Iron, Fiber and Phosphorus

Pasta Salad

Ingredients:

1 lb spiral pasta noodles (a variety of flavors is good)
8 oz. chicken, cubed or 8 oz. peeled shrimp or 8 oz. cubed ham
1 small onion, chopped
1 stalk celery, chopped
1 large carrot, chopped
1 cup fresh broccoli, chopped
1 cup fresh cauliflower, chopped
1 small red bell pepper, chopped
1/2 cup fresh mushrooms, sliced
Other vegetables as desired ie: corn, peas, cucumbers…
1 16 oz. bottle fat free Italian dressing

Directions:

Cook noodles according to package directions until tender. Cook chicken until tender in small amount of water, and cube. Add chicken, vegetables and dressing to noodles and toss. Chill for 1 hr. Serves 8.

Nutrition Information:

Total calories	Total grams protein	Total grams carbohydrate	Total grams fat
289	10	41	4.5

Significant source of the following vitamins, minerals and other nutrients:

Vitamins A, C, Thiamin, Riboflavin, Niacin, Potassium, Iron, fiber and Phosphorus

Bunny Foxhoven, R.D.

Pasta Salad Primavera

Ingredients:

8 oz. whole wheat or spinach pasta shells or spirals
1 carrot, sliced thin
1 cup asparagus, chopped
1 cup zucchini, cut into thin strips
1 cup fresh mushrooms, sliced
1 each red and yellow bell pepper, chopped
1 t. mustard
1/3 cup fat free Italian dressing
1/3 cup shredded parmesan cheese
2 T. parsley
2 T. basil

Directions:

Make pasta according to package, drain and put in large bowl, add all ingredients and toss to coat with dressing. Serve chilled or at room temperature. Serves 4.

Nutrition Information:

Total calories	Total grams protein	Total grams carbohydrate	Total grams fat
290	9	30	3

Significant source of the following vitamins, minerals and other nutrients:

Vitamins A, C, Thiamin, Riboflavin, Niacin, Potassium, Iron, fiber and Phosphorus

Pasta Crab Salad

Ingredients:

8 oz pkg. pasta spirals, preferably mixed vegetable flavors
8 oz. cooked crab meat, or use shrimp or poultry
1 large mild onion
1/2 c. fat free mayonnaise or miracle whip
1 large tomato, chopped
1/2 cup broccoli, chopped
1/2 cup cauliflower, chopped
1/2 cup carrots, chopped
1/4 cup celery, chopped

Directions:

Boil pasta until tender, drain and rinse with cold water. Add all other ingredients and toss lightly, chill. Makes 10 1/2 cup servings.

Nutrition Information:

Total calories	Total grams protein	Total grams carbohydrate	Total grams fat
144	9	25	1

Significant source of the following vitamins, minerals and other nutrients:

Vitamins A, C, Thiamin, Niacin, Iron and Fiber

Bunny Foxhoven, R.D.

Oriental Chicken Salad

Ingredients:

Salad:
1 lb. chicken breasts
1 med. head Iceberg lettuce
2 stalks celery
1 cup fresh broccoli, chopped
1 cup Chinese bean sprouts
1/4 c. cashews
1 16 oz. can mandarin oranges or seedless grapes

Dressing:
1/4 c. salad type mustard
1/2 c. honey

Directions:

Cook chicken in small amount of water until tender. chop into small strips or chunks. Chop vegetables and in large bowl toss all ingredients, including dressing. Chill 1 hour. serves 8.

Nutrition Information:

Total calories	Total grams protein	Total grams carbohydrate	Total grams fat
146	16	9	4

Significant source of the following vitamins, minerals and other nutrients:

Calcium, Niacin, Potassium, Phosphorus, Iron and Fiber

Taco Salad

Ingredients:

2 heads iceberg lettuce (or others if desired), chopped
4 whole tomatoes, chopped
32 oz. chunky salsa
16 oz pinto beans in chili sauce
1 lb. lean ground beef
8 oz. nonfat plain yogurt
8 oz. nonfat or low fat cheddar cheese, shredded
1 package chili seasoning powder
8 oz. no fat chips

Directions:

Brown ground beef in skillet, drain off all grease (rinse if desired to remove all fat), add pinto beans and chili seasoning and heat through. Top lettuce and tomatoes with meat/bean mixture, salsa, yogurt, cheese and chips. Serves 8.

Nutrition Information:

Total calories	Total grams protein	Total grams carbohydrate	Total grams fat
477	30	44	20

Significant source of the following vitamins, minerals and other nutrients:

Vitamins A, C, Thiamin, Iron, Potassium, Calcium Lycopene and Fiber

Bunny Foxhoven, R.D.

Chapter 23

Super Side Dishes

1. Confetti Cabbage
2. Creamy Garlic Potatoes
3. Lemon Potato Wedges
4. Twice Baked Potatoes
5. Best Potato Salad
6. Lemon Rice
7. Creole Rice
8. Confetti Rice
9. Black Beans and Rice
10. Lemon Couscous
11. Delicious Baked Beans

Lemon Potato Wedges

Ingredients:

6 medium baking potatoes
1 1/2 t lemon rind, grated
2 T. lemon juice
1 1/2 dill
1/4 c. parmesan cheese, grated

Directions:

Wash and cut potatoes into wedges, Toss with lemon rind, lemon juice and dill, place in baking dish and top with cheese. Bake 350 degrees for 30 minutes or until potatoes are soft. Makes 8 1/2 c. servings.

Nutrition Information:

Total calories	Total grams protein	Total grams carbohydrate	Total grams fat
88	3	17	1

Significant source of the following vitamins, minerals and other nutrients:

Vitamins A, C and Calcium

Bunny Foxhoven, R.D.

Twice Baked Potatoes

Ingredients:

4 large baked potatoes
8 oz shredded nonfat cheddar cheese
2 T. milk
dash pepper
2 T. chives, chopped

Directions:

Bake potatoes to tender 6 minutes in microwave or 25 in oven. Cut in half and remove most of potato from skin. Mash potatoes with other ingredients and place back in skins. Bake for 20 minutes. Serves 8

Nutrition Information:

Total calories	Total grams protein	Total grams carbohydrate	Total grams fat
36	6	3	4

Significant source of the following vitamins, minerals and other nutrients:

Vitamin C and Calcium

Best Potato Salad

Ingredients:

4 - medium potatoes washed and cubed
1/2 cup plain nonfat yogurt
1/4 cup fat free mayonnaise
1 t. tarragon
1 T. vinegar
1 t. mustard

Directions:

Boil potato cubes until firm but tender, Mix in all other ingredients gently. Serve hot or cold. Makes 6 1/2 cup servings.

Nutrition Information:

Total calories	Total grams protein	Total grams carbohydrate	Total grams fat
115	2	18	3

Significant source of the following vitamins, minerals and other nutrients:

Calcium, Potassium and Phosphorus

Bunny Foxhoven, R.D.

Lemon Rice

Ingredients:

1/2 clove garlic, minced
4 cups boiling water
1 chicken bouillon cube
1 1/2 cup cooked brown rice
2 T. parsley, chopped
1 T. lemon juice
1 t. lemon rind, grated

Directions:

Dissolve bouillon cube in water, add garlic, bring to boil add rice and boil 15 to 20 minutes, reduce heat and cover, let simmer 20 more minutes until water is absorbed, stir in parsley, lemon and rind. Serve warm. Makes 4 1/2 servings.

Nutrition Information:

Total calories	Total grams protein	Total grams carbohydrate	Total grams fat
91	1	20	0

Significant source of the following vitamins, minerals and other nutrients:

Vitamin A, Thiamin, Riboflavin, Niacin and Fiber

Creole Rice

Ingredients:

1 c. rice, uncooked
1/2 c. onion, chopped
1/2 c. green pepper, chopped
1 14 oz. can stewed tomatoes with juice
1 t. parsley flakes
1/2 t garlic powder
1/2 t. oregano
1/2 t. salt

Directions:

Using juice of tomatoes an part of the water to cook rice, add uncooked rice and all ingredients in pan and cook according to rice instructions. Makes 8 1/2 cup servings.

Nutrition Information:

Total calories	Total grams protein	Total grams carbohydrate	Total grams fat
90	1	20	0

Significant source of the following vitamins, minerals and other nutrients:

Vitamins A, C and Calcium

Bunny Foxhoven, R.D.

Confetti Rice

Ingredients:

1 c. uncooked long cooking rice
1/2 c. onion, chopped
1 1/2 c. water
3 chicken bouillon cubes (dissolve in water)
1/2 c. dry wine or sherry
2 1/2 small cans of chopped mushrooms or 1 c. chopped
1 20 oz. jar pimentos
fresh mushrooms
1/2 t. salt
1/2 t. pepper
1/2 t. garlic powder

Directions:

Cook rice according to package. While rice cooks sauté onions, mushrooms and pimentos in wine and spices. Toss all ingredients together and serve. Makes 8 1/2 cup servings.

Nutrition Information:

Total calories Total grams protein Total grams carbohydrate Total grams fat
116   2   23   0

Significant source of the following vitamins, minerals and other nutrients:

Vitamins A, C and Calcium

Black Beans and Rice

Ingredients:

1 c. rice, uncooked
1 15 oz. can black beans, drained
3/4 c. tomatoes, chopped
1 t. red wine vinegar
1 c. onion, chopped
1/2 c. green pepper, chopped
1/2 t. cumin or 1/4 c. fresh cilantro
1/8 t. red pepper
1/2 t. coriander

Directions:

Cook rice according to package. Add remaining ingredients together and mix with cooked rice. Serve hot. Makes 6 1/2 c. servings.

Nutrition Information:

Total calories	Total grams protein	Total grams carbohydrate	Total grams fat
186	6	38	0

Significant source of the following vitamins, minerals and other nutrients:

Vitamins A, C, Calcium and Lycopene

Bunny Foxhoven, R.D.

Lemon Couscous

Ingredients:

1 1/3 c. couscous, uncooked
2 1/4 water
1/3 c. green onion, chopped
1/4 t. salt
2 1/4 t. grated lemon rind

Directions:

Mix all ingredients and cook until water is absorbed and couscous are soft. Makes 8 1/2 c. servings.

Nutrition Information:

Total calories	Total grams protein	Total grams carbohydrate	Total grams fat
146	5	30	0

Significant source of the following vitamins, minerals and other nutrients:

Vitamin A and Calcium

Delicious Baked Beans

Ingredients:

1 16 oz package dry navy beans
1 1/2 qt. water
2 c. onion, chopped
1 c. catsup
1/2 c. lean ham, dices
1/2 c. molasses
1 T. prepared mustard
1/2 t. salt
1/2 t. pepper

Directions:

Bring beans and water to rapid boil, remove from heat and set soak overnight. Bring beans and water back to boil and simmer for 2 hrs. All remaining ingredients and bake in qt. dish at 350 degrees for 1 hr. Makes 15 1/2 c. servings.

Nutrition Information:

Total calories	Total grams protein	Total grams carbohydrate	Total grams fat
166	8	32	0

Significant source of the following vitamins, minerals and other nutrients:

Vitamin A, Calcium and Fiber

Bunny Foxhoven, R.D.

Chapter 24

In from the Orient

1. Sesame Snow Peas
2. Teri Chicken and Vegetables
3. Teriyaki Chicken Kabobs
4. Stir Fry Chicken and Vegetables
5. Oriental Shrimp and Snow Peas
6. Chop Suey

Sesame Snow Peas

Ingredients:

3/4 lb snow peas
2 large red bell peppers, cut in strips
1/2 c. onion, chopped
1 T. sesame seeds
1/2 t. Mrs. or Papa Dash type herb seasoning mix

Directions:

Sauté snow peas, peppers and onions in non stick pan with non stick spray or coating. Toss with spices and serve. Makes 10 1/2 c. servings.

Nutrition Information:

Total calories	Total grams protein	Total grams carbohydrate	Total grams fat
26	0	3	1

Significant source of the following vitamins, minerals and other nutrients:

Vitamins A, C, E and Fiber

Bunny Foxhoven, R.D.

Teriyaki Chicken and Vegetables

Ingredients:

1 cup each: Broccoli
Cauliflower
Carrots
Chinese bean sprouts
Celery
Snow pea pods
Purple cabbage
any other vegetable you like!
1 clove garlic, minced
1 two inch piece fresh ginger root, minced
4 boneless, skinless chicken breasts, cubed
2 cubes chicken bullion
cornstarch to thicken broth

Directions:

In wok or large skillet cook chicken cubes in 4 c. water until cooked through. Add garlic, ginger, sherry and bullion. Prepare a cornstarch water paste using 2 T. cornstarch and 1/4 c. cold water. Slowly stir into chicken and water. Remove from pan and set aside. Place chopped carrots, cauliflower, and broccoli stalks into pan and cook 3 - 5 minutes, stirring often. Add remaining vegetables and cook 3 - 5 more minutes until slightly tender but still crunchy. Add chicken and sauce back to pan and heat through, approximately 3 minutes. Serve over whole grain, long cooking brown rice. Serves 8, 1 c. each.

Nutrition Information:

Total calories	Total grams protein	Total grams carbohydrate	Total grams fat
169	28	6	1

Significant source of the following vitamins, minerals and other nutrients:

Vitamin A, Vitamin C, Calcium and fiber

Bunny Foxhoven, R.D.

Teriyaki Chicken Kabobs

Ingredients:

4 Boneless, skinless, cubed chicken breasts
2 large green bell peppers
16 cherry tomatoes
1 medium onion, cut into wedges and separated
1 cup fresh or canned pineapple chunks
1/2 c. teriyaki marinade, jar or use stir fry recipe

Directions:

Cook chicken in 2 cups water and teriyaki sauce until tender. Alternate peppers, chicken, pineapple, onion, and tomatoes. Cook on barbeque grill or in large skillet approximately 10 minutes or until tomatoes are softened. Makes 16 kabobs.

Nutrition Information:

Total calories	Total grams protein	Total grams carbohydrate	Total grams fat
169	28	6	1

Significant source of the following vitamins, minerals and other nutrients:

Vitamins A, C, Calcium, Fiber and Lycopene

Stir Fry Chicken and Vegetables

Ingredients:

4 Boned, Skinned and cubed chicken breasts
1/2 c. diced onion
2 minced garlic cloves
1 2" piece ginger root, minced
1/4 c. light soy sauce
1/4 c. saki or sherry
2 chicken bouillon
1 cup each:
    chopped broccoli
    sliced carrots
    chopped cauliflower
    chopped purple cabbage
    chopped celery
    bean sprouts
    snow pea pods

Directions:

In wok or large skillet cook chicken in about 2 cups water to tender, add water if it evaporates out. Add onion, garlic, cloves and bouillon, simmer 15 minutes. Add broccoli stems, carrots and cauliflower, cook 10 minutes. Add all remaining vegetables, soy sauce and saki or sherry and heat through. Serve over whole grain rice. serves 8.

Nutrition Information:

Total calories	Total grams protein	Total grams carbohydrate	Total grams fat
173	29	6	1

Bunny Foxhoven, R.D.

Significant source of the following vitamins, minerals and other nutrients:

Vitamins A, C, Calcium and Fiber

Oriental Shrimp and Snow Peas

Ingredients:

1 1/2 lb. peeled and de-veined medium shrimp
6 oz. frozen snow peas (1 package)
1/4 c. green onion, chopped
1 clove garlic, minced
1 t. ginger
1/8 t. pepper
1 1/2 c. water
3 chicken bouillon, dissolved in water
1 1/2 T. cornstarch
1/8 t. thyme

Directions:

Cook onion, garlic and shrimp in non stick pan for 3 minutes, stirring constantly. Stir in vegetables, ginger and bouillon. Cover and simmer for 7 minutes. Dissolve cornstarch in 1/2 cup water and slowly add to pan, stirring constantly. Sprinkle with thyme and serve over rice or oriental noodles. Makes 4 servings.

Nutrition Information:

Total calories	Total grams protein	Total grams carbohydrate	Total grams fat
214	35	8	3

Significant source of the following vitamins, minerals and other nutrients:

Vitamins A, C, Iron, Calcium and Potassium

Bunny Foxhoven, R.D.

Chop Suey

Ingredients:

8 oz. cooked turkey breast, cut into strips
1 1/2 t. thyme
1 large head cabbage, shredded
3 c. shredded carrots
3 large tomatoes, chopped
1 medium onion thinly sliced
1/2 t. black pepper
1/2 t. salt
1/4 c. water

Directions:

In wok or large skillet add all ingredients, Mix well and cook covered until vegetables become tender, stirring often. It becomes more tender as it cooks. Serves 10.

Nutrition Information:

Total calories	Total grams protein	Total grams carbohydrate	Total grams fat
72	7	10	0

Significant source of the following vitamins, minerals and other nutrients:

Vitamins A, C, Calcium and Fiber

Chapter 25

A Taste of Italy

1. Spaghetti Sauce
2. Hearty Calzones
3. Italian Dough for Pizza and Calzones
4. Heart-y Pizza
5. Traditional Gnocchi
6. Spinach Gnocchi
7. Spaghetti Carbonarra
8. Greek Capellini
9. Linguini in Cream Sauce
10. Eggplant Parmesan
11. Pisto
12. Zucchini Linguini
13. Vegetarian Lasagna
14. Any Way Lasagna
15. Chicken Parmesan
16. Chicken Fettuccini
17. Low Fat Italian Sausage

Bunny Foxhoven, R.D.

Spaghetti Sauce

Ingredients:

1 med. Onion, chopped
2 cloves garlic, minced
1 large bell pepper, chopped
5 large mushrooms, chopped
2 bay leaves
2 bouillon cubes
1 16 oz. can tomato sauce
1 32 oz. can whole tomatoes
1/4 t. rosemary
1/2 t. thyme
1/2 t. basil
1 t. oregano
1/4 t. black peppe
1 lb. extra lean ground beef, turkey or Italian sausage (optional)
1 t. sugar (optional)

Directions:

    Brown meat in large sauce pan, drain (if no meat is used add some of the tomato sauce) sauté onions, peppers and garlic. Add remaining ingredients and simmer 1 1/2 hours, stirring occasionally. Serves 6. Some ideas for using this sauce:
        Franzis or other low fat raviolis
        Tortellini
        Whole grain or spinach noodles (any shape)
        Use in several of the Italian recipes in this cookbook.

Nutrition Information:

Total calories	Total grams protein	Total grams carbohydrate	Total grams fat
124	15	11	3

Significant source of the following vitamins, minerals and other nutrients:

Vitamins A, C, Thiamin, Riboflavin, Lycopene

Bunny Foxhoven, R.D.

Heart-Y-Calzones

Ingredients:

1 recipe for calzone dough
1 cup spaghetti sauce (see recipe)
4 oz. fat free mozzarella cheese
1/2 cup onion, chopped
1 cup green bell pepper, chopped
1 cup mushrooms, sliced
1 cup broccoli or zucchini (optional)
1 lb. homemade sausage (see recipe)

Directions:

Prepare Dough as directed in recipe. Brown sausage in skillet and drain off excess grease. Roll out dough into 6 small circles. Spread 1/6 of sauce on dough and put 1/6 of sausage, cheese and vegetables on one side fold over and pinch edges together, you may need to moisten the edge to make them stick. bake on cookie sheet at 450 degrees for 10 minutes or until brown. Makes 6 large calzones.

Nutrition Information:

Total calories	Total grams protein	Total grams carbohydrate	Total grams fat
459	32	57	10

Significant source of the following vitamins, minerals and other nutrients:

Vitamins A, C, Thiamin, Riboflavin, Niacin, Iron, Calcium and Fiber

Italian Dough for Pizza and Calzones

Ingredients:

1/4 cup warm water
1 T. active dry yeast
3 cups whole wheat pastry flour
1 t. salt
1 t. basil
1 t. oregano
3/4 cup cool water
1 t. sugar or honey
2 T. olive oil

Directions:

Dissolve yeast in warm water and let stand until small bubbles begin to form. Combine and mix flour and seasonings. Combine sugar or honey and oil in cool water, then add yeast. Slowly stir in flour mixture and mix until forms a large ball. Knead on lightly floured surface for about 10 minutes until soft and elastic. Place dough in greased bowl, cover and let rise in warm dry area for 1 hour. Punch down in center and let stand for 10 minutes, cut in half for two pizza crusts or in fourths for calzones and roll out to approximately 1/4 inch thick. Top as desired. See heart-y-pizza or calzone recipes for ideas. Makes 2 12 inch pizzas or 4 large calzones.

Nutrition Information:

Total calories	Total grams protein	Total grams carbohydrate	Total grams fat
125	4	22	2

Bunny Foxhoven, R.D.

Significant source of the following vitamins, minerals and other nutrients:

Thiamin, Riboflavin, Niacin and Fiber

Heart-Y-Pizza

Ingredients:

16 ounces whole wheat bread dough (or 1 pizza crust of your choice)
8 ounces pizza or spaghetti sauce (no meat or cheese added)
8 ounces Canadian bacon, sliced
8 ounces non fat mozzarella cheese
1 green bell pepper, chopped
1 small onion, chopped
1/2 cup sliced black olives
1 cup sliced mushrooms

Directions:

Roll dough into cookie pan, bake for 10 minutes at 375 degrees.
Spread pizza sauce over crust leaving edge for crusts. Layer meat, veggies and then cheese over crust, bake for 15 minutes at 375, turn on broiler for a few minutes if browned cheese is desired. Watch carefully so it doesn't burn if you use broiler!

Nutrition Information:

Total calories	Total grams protein	Total grams carbohydrate	Total grams fat
197	13	22	6

Significant source of the following vitamins, minerals and other nutrients:

Vitamins A, C Thiamin, Riboflavin, Niacin Calcium and Fiber

Bunny Foxhoven, R.D.

Traditional Gnocchi

Ingredients:

2 c. boiled and mashed potatoes (can use instant but fresh is best, peels may be removed if desired but decreases nutritional value of potato!)
2/3 c. parmesan cheese
2 eggs
1/4 c. whole wheat pastry flour
1/4 t. black pepper
1/8 t. salt
2 c. favorite spaghetti sauce

Directions:

Cook potatoes until tender, drain and mash or press in garlic press. Mix potatoes, pepper and salt in sauce pan, heat 5 minutes. Remove from heat and add flour, eggs, and 1/2 cheese. Fold in with hands and shape into 1/2 inch balls. Lower gnocchi's into 4 - 6 quarts boiling water. When gnocchi's puff up and float to the top remove with slotted spoon. Serve with spaghetti sauce and sprinkle with remaining parmesan cheese. Makes 42 1/2 inch gnocchi's.

Nutrition Information:

Total calories	Total grams protein	Total grams carbohydrate	Total grams fat
116	5	16	3

Significant source of the following vitamins, minerals and other nutrients:

Vitamin A, Calcium and Fiber

Spinach Gnocchi

Ingredients:

1 c. finely chopped spinach, thawed and drained (can be fresh or frozen)
8 oz. dry curd cottage cheese
2/3 c. parmesan cheese
2 eggs
1 c. whole wheat pastry flour
1/4 t. black pepper
1/8 t. nutmeg
2 c. of your favorite spaghetti sauce

Directions:

Cook spinach until tender, drain and squeeze excess water off. Mix spinach, cottage cheese, pepper and nutmeg in sauce pan, heat 5 minutes. Remove from heat and add flour, eggs, and 1/2 cheese. Fold in with hands and shape into 1 inch balls. Lower gnocchi balls into 4 - 6 quarts boiling water. When gnocchi's puff up and float to the top, remove with slotted spoon. Serve topped with spaghetti sauce and sprinkle with remaining parmesan cheese. Makes 24 1 inch gnocchi's.

Nutrition Information:

Total calories	Total grams protein	Total grams carbohydrate	Total grams fat
142	10	18	3

Significant source of the following vitamins, minerals and other nutrients:

Vitamins A, C, Calcium and Fiber

Bunny Foxhoven, R.D.

Spaghetti Carbonara

Ingredients:

1 large onion, chopped
3 cloves garlic, minced
4 - 6 oz. Canadian bacon, diced
1/2 cup skim milk
2 eggs
1/4 t. pepper
1/2 pound of your favorite noodles
4 t. parmesan cheese

Directions:

In large pan boil 4 quarts water, add spaghetti noodles and cook until just tender. Do not over cook.

Meanwhile, Sauté onion and garlic in nonstick skillet and a small amount of water. Add bacon and cook 5 minutes. In small bowl beat eggs and milk together, pour into saucepan. heat until it thickens. Toss into cooked noodles and top with parmesan cheese. Makes 4 1 cup servings.

Nutrition Information:

Total calories	Total grams protein	Total grams carbohydrate	Total grams fat
350	21	47	8

Significant source of the following vitamins, minerals and other nutrients:

Vitamin A, Calcium and Fiber

Greek Capellini

Ingredients:

6 oz. uncooked Angel Hair Pasta
1 lb. fresh broccoli, chopped
1/2 t. fresh minced garlic
1/2 c. water
1 chicken bouillon cube, dissolve in water
2 c. tomatoes, chopped
1/3 c. feta cheese

Directions:

Cook pasta according to directions. Add remaining ingredients together. Toss over pasta and sprinkle with cheese. Makes 7 1/2 c. servings.

Nutrition Information:

Total calories	Total grams protein	Total grams carbohydrate	Total grams fat
146	6	26	2

Significant source of the following vitamins, minerals and other nutrients:

Vitamins A, C, Calcium and Lycopene

Bunny Foxhoven, R.D.

Linguini in Cream Sauce

Ingredients:

6 oz linguini, uncooked
1/4 c. nonfat yogurt
1 1/3 c. mushrooms, chopped
1/2 c. onions, chopped
1 1/2 T. Parmesan Cheese, grated
1/8 t. salt
1/8 t. pepper
1 T. parsley, chopped

Directions:

Cook pasta according to package. Combine remaining ingredients and warm but do not bring to boil. Toss into pasta and sprinkle with parsley. Makes 4 3/4 servings.

Nutrition Information:

Total calories	Total grams protein	Total grams carbohydrate	Total grams fat
348	22	36	12

Significant source of the following vitamins, minerals and other nutrients:

Vitamin A and Calcium

Eggplant Parmesan

Ingredients:

1 large eggplant, cut into rounds
1 28 oz. cans tomato puree
1 T. plus 1/4 t. oregano
16 oz. 1 % cottage cheese
1 clove garlic
1/4 t. garlic powder
2 T. whole wheat flour
4 oz part skim mozzarella cheese, grated

Directions:

Cut eggplant and place in 1/2 inch water in steamer or boiling pot. steam for 10 minutes. Meanwhile combine tomato puree, oregano and garlic in bowl. In another bowl combine cottage cheese, flour, 1/4 t. oregano and 1/4 t. garlic powder. In large baking dish lay out eggplant wedges. Top with sauce then cottage cheese then sauce. Top with cheese and bake at 350 for 20 minutes. Makes 4 large servings.

Nutrition Information:

Total calories	Total grams protein	Total grams carbohydrate	Total grams fat
331	28	42	7

Significant source of the following vitamins, minerals and other nutrients:

Vitamins A, C, Calcium, Fiber and Lycopene

Bunny Foxhoven, R.D.

Pisto

Ingredients:

12 oz cooked lean ham, cut into strips
2 large onions, sliced
2 garlic cloves, minced
1 medium green pepper, diced
10 oz. Package of frozen green beans or lima beans
9 oz. marinated artichoke hearts, drained
1 16 oz can whole peeled tomatoes

Directions:

Sauté ham, onions, garlic and green pepper in Teflon pan, use 1/4 cup water if it is sticking, add remaining ingredients and cover and simmer for 15 minutes. Makes 4 1/2 cup servings.

Nutrition Information:

Total calories	Total grams protein	Total grams carbohydrate	Total grams fat
242	23	26	6

Significant source of the following vitamins, minerals and other nutrients:

Vitamins A, C, Thiamin, Fiber and Lycopene

Zucchini Linguini

Ingredients:

1 medium onion, chopped
4 cloves garlic, minced
8 cups zucchini cubes, from 8 medium zucchinis
16 oz linguini noodles
28 oz can whole peeled tomatoes or 8 fresh cubed tomatoes
salt and pepper to taste
parmesan cheese topping

Directions:

In non stick skillet sauté' onion and garlic in small amount of water until soft. Add zucchini and sauté 20 minutes. Add tomatoes and seasoning to taste, heat additional 5 minutes. Boil linguini in large pan of water until tender during the time the zucchini cooks, drain. Serve zucchini sauce over linguini. Makes 8 cups noodles and 8 cups sauce.

Nutrition Information:

Total calories	Total grams protein	Total grams carbohydrate	Total grams fat
259	10	52	1

Significant source of the following vitamins, minerals and other nutrients:

Vitamin A, C, Calcium, Fiber and Lycopene

Bunny Foxhoven, R.D.

Veggie Lasagna

Ingredients:

8 oz. package lasagna noodles
16 oz frozen mixed vegetables, broccoli, cauliflower, carrots…
(or 4 cups fresh chopped)
10 package frozen chopped spinach
1 medium onion, chopped
16 oz. 1 % cottage cheese
8 oz. can chopped mushrooms
32 oz. spaghetti sauce
6 oz. mozzarella cheese

Directions:

Boil lasagna noodles in large pan until tender. Lay lengthwise in 9 x 13 baking pan. Begin layering all ingredients: Noodles, sauce, vegetables, cottage cheese, repeat until all ingredients are used up. Bake at 350 for 45 - 50 minutes. Top with mozzarella cheese. Makes 12 servings.

Nutrition Information:

Total calories	Total grams protein	Total grams carbohydrate	Total grams fat
178	9	26	4

Significant source of the following vitamins, minerals and other nutrients:

Vitamins A, C, Calcium, Fiber and Lycopene

Any Way Lasagna

Ingredients:

1 16 OZ. package spinach, whole wheat or regular lasagna noodles
64 OZ. Spaghetti Sauce
16 OZ 1% cottage cheese
8 oz. Nonfat or low fat mozzarella cheese
1 lb lean ground turkey, browned and drained
    or
1 package tofu, drained
    or
2 lb fresh or frozen vegetable combinations (broccoli, cauliflower, carrots, peas, corn, lima beans, squash, onions, mushrooms...
    or
2 10 oz. boxes frozen spinach or fresh, chopped spinach

Directions:

Layer; noodles, sauce, cottage cheese, meat/tofu or vegetables, repeat, top off with mozzarella. Bake 350 for 30-45 minutes.
Serves 12.

Nutrition Information:

Total calories	Total grams protein	Total grams carbohydrate	Total grams fat
221	19	21	5

Significant source of the following vitamins, minerals and other nutrients:

Vitamin A, Calcium and Lycopene

Bunny Foxhoven, R.D.

Chicken Parmesan

Ingredients:

4 large boneless, skinless chicken breasts
4 oz. nonfat mozzarella cheese (specialty item)
1/5 c. spaghetti sauce

Directions:

Place chicken in baking dish, place spaghetti sauce and 1 oz. mozzarella cheese on each chicken breast. bake 40-45 minutes on 350. Serves 4.

Nutrition Information:

Total calories	Total grams protein	Total grams carbohydrate	Total grams fat
349	62	3	8

Significant source of the following vitamins, minerals and other nutrients:

Vitamin A, Calcium and Lycopene

Chicken Fettuccini

Ingredients:

1 Lb. boneless skinless chicken breast, cubed (4 small breast)
12 medium mushrooms, sliced
2 cup spaghetti marinara
1 8 oz package whole wheat or regular fettuccini noodles
parmesan cheese to top

Directions:

Boil cubed chicken in small amount of water in skillet to brown. Add mushrooms and wine, cook until all liquid evaporates. Add spaghetti sauce and simmer for 10 minutes. Meanwhile boil noodles until tender and drain. Place noodles in large bowl, pour in sauce and toss gently to cover all noodles. Serve topped with parmesan cheese. Makes 4 1 cup servings.

Nutrition Information:

Total calories	Total grams protein	Total grams carbohydrate	Total grams fat
429	36	53	5

Significant source of the following vitamins, minerals and other nutrients:

Vitamin A, Calcium, Iron and Lycopene

Bunny Foxhoven, R.D.

Low Fat Italian Sausage

Ingredients:

1 lb. lean ground turkey, beef or pork (should be 93% lean or greater)
1 t. fennel seeds, crushed
1/2 t. oregano
1 t. basil
1/4 t. salt
2 garlic cloves, minced or 1 t. garlic paste

Directions:

In bowl combine all ingredients and mix with hands until blended, cover and place in refrigerator overnight to enhance flavor.

Nutrition Information:

Total calories	Total grams protein	Total grams carbohydrate	Total grams fat
125	28	3	0

Significant source of the following vitamins, minerals and other nutrients:

Thiamin and Iron

Chapter 26
South of the Border

1. Mexican Pizza Squares for Kids
2. Chili Rellenos Without the Fat
3. Super Green Chili
4. Smothered Green Chili Burritos
5. Mexican Green Rice Casserole
6. Southwestern Spicy Stir Fry
7. Chicken and Spinach Enchiladas
8. Tacos With a Twist
9. Mexican Potato Skins
10. Chicken Wonderful
11. Chicken Fajitas
12. Chicken Enchiladas
13. Amigo Pie

Bunny Foxhoven, R.D.

Mexican Pizza Squares for Kids

Ingredients:

1/2 cup cornmeal
1 T/ baking powder
1 1/2 cup whole wheat pastry flour
1/2 t. salt
3/4 cup skim milk
1/4 cup oil
1/2 lb. lean ground beef or turkey
1 small green pepper, cut in rings
8 oz low fat mozzarella cheese
8 oz. mild taco sauce or tomato sauce

Directions:

In bowl mix cornmeal, flour, baking powder, salt, milk and oil. Mix well, press into greased 9 x 9 inch pan. Bake crust 10 minutes Spread tomato sauce over crust, top with meat, peppers and cheese. bake 5 minutes. Makes 9 child sized slices.

Nutrition Information:

Total calories	Total grams protein	Total grams carbohydrate	Total grams fat
273	15	25	12

Significant source of the following vitamins, minerals and other nutrients:

Vitamin A, Calcium, Fiber and Lycopene

Super Green Chili

Ingredients:

2 lb. boneless skinless chicken or lean pork
2 1/2 c. water
1/2 c. chopped onion
2 cloves minced garlic
1/2 c. whole wheat pastry flour
1 16 oz. whole peeled tomatoes
2 7 oz. cans diced green chilies, choose the spiciest you like
1/4 t. cumin

Directions:

Cube meat and put in large 5 quart kettle with 1/2 c. water, cook until meat browns and water evaporates. Add onion, garlic and flour, stir until meat is coated with flour, add remaining water and other ingredients and bring to boil, cover and reduce heat and simmer for 1 hour. Makes 8 1 cup bowls for stew or smoothers 16 burritos.

Nutrition Information:

Total calories	Total grams protein	Total grams carbohydrate	Total grams fat
122	14	12	2

Significant source of the following vitamins, minerals and other nutrients:

Vitamin A, Fiber and Lycopene

Bunny Foxhoven, R.D.

Smothered Green Chili Burritos

Green Chili Ingredients:

2 boneless skinless chicken breasts
1/4 c. flour
64 oz. canned whole peeled tomatoes or fresh chopped tomatoes
8 oz tomato sauce
8 oz chopped jalapeno peppers or chili peppers
1/4 c. fresh chopped cilantro or cumin
1/4 t. pepper
1/4 t. garlic powder or 1 chopped garlic clove
Extra flour for thickening

Burrito Ingredients:

6 Whole wheat flour tortillas
16 oz. generic refried beans (check the label, they have no fat!)
1 lb. Lean ground turkey or beef
3 oz. nonfat plain yogurt
3 oz. nonfat or low fat cheddar cheese
Lettuce and tomatoes to top

Directions:

    Chop chicken into cubes, place in large pan, add 1 c. water and cook on high until chicken is cooked through and water evaporates. Sprinkle 1/4 c. flour onto chicken and coat. Add about 1/4 c. cold water to chicken to make flour paste. Add tomatoes, sauce, peppers, and spices. Cook on low for 1 hour or more. Add more flour/water paste to thicken if desired. It becomes spicier as it cooks. To prepare the burritos brown the ground turkey. In each tortilla spread: 1/6th of the turkey, 1/6th of the beans, 1/2 oz yogurt, 1/2 oz. cheese and roll. Place in a baking dish and smoother with green chili. Bake 30 minutes on 350. Serve topped with lettuce and tomatoes and no fat chips.

Nutrition Information:

Total calories Total grams protein Total grams carbohydrate Total grams fat
264   19   27   8

Significant source of the following vitamins, minerals and other nutrients:

Vitamin A, Calcium and Fiber

Bunny Foxhoven, R.D.

Mexican Green Rice Casserole

Ingredients:

8 cups brown rice, cooked
1 cup nonfat plain yogurt
1/2 cup chopped green chilies
1 1/2 cup fat free cheddar cheese, grated

Directions:

Cook rice according to package, combine remaining ingredients and stir together. Bake at 350 degrees for 15 minutes until bubbly. Makes 8 servings.

Nutrition Information:

Total calories	Total grams protein	Total grams carbohydrate	Total grams fat
266	8	47	4

Significant source of the following vitamins, minerals and other nutrients:

Vitamin A, Thiamin and Calcium

Southwestern Spicy Stir Fry

Ingredients:

8 oz. chicken breast or lean beef strips
2 t. cornstarch
1 chicken bouillon
1/2 c. cooked pinto or black beans
2 jalapeno or green chilies, chopped
1 medium onion, chopped
1 15 oz. can baby corn
1 medium zucchini, sliced
1 small jicama, sliced
1 medium red or yellow bell pepper, sliced
1 T. lime juice
dash cumin
1/2 t. salt
1/2 t. oregano
1/4 c. cilantro, finely chopped

Directions:

Marinate meat in bowl containing; lime juice, cumin, oregano, salt and cilantro, let stand. Mix cornstarch and bouillon in 1/2 c. water. Heat wok to high and add garlic, beans, chilies and meat and stir fry until meat is just browned, add onion and jicama and cook for 1 minute, add remaining vegetables and broth and cook for two additional minutes. Stir once to mix well and cover and cook until sauce thickens. Serves 3.

Nutrition Information:

Total calories	Total grams protein	Total grams carbohydrate	Total grams fat
107	11	13	0

Bunny Foxhoven, R.D.

Significant source of the following vitamins, minerals and other nutrients:

Vitamins A, C, Thiamin, Riboflavin, Niacin, Potassium, Iron, fiber and Phosphorus

Chicken and Spinach Enchiladas

Ingredients:

1 10 oz. package frozen chopped spinach, thawed and drained or 1 cup fresh, cooked spinach
3/4 cup 1% cottage cheese
1 4 oz. can diced green chilies
1 lb. chicken breasts, skinned, and cubed
1 19 oz can enchilada sauce
8 corn tortillas
2 oz. fat free cheddar cheese
1/2 cup nonfat plain yogurt
1/4 t. cumin
1/4 t. dried oregano
2 green onions, sliced

Directions:

Squeeze excess water off spinach and in one bowl mix spinach, cottage cheese, green chilies, oregano and cumin. In skillet boil chicken cubes in small amount of water to cook through. Place 1/4 of enchilada sauce in wide flat bowl and lay tortillas one at a time in sauce to coat both sides. Coat bottom of 9 x 13 inch baking dish with 1 T. enchilada sauce and begin making enchiladas one at a time by placing 1/4 cup spinach and 1/4 cup chicken in center of tortilla then roll tortilla to close. Place on flap side down and line up in pan. Pour on remaining sauce and top with cheese. Cover with foil and bake for 30 minutes at 375 degrees until bubbly. Place 1 T. yogurt and onions on top. Makes 8 enchiladas.

Nutrition Information:

Total calories	Total grams protein	Total grams carbohydrate	Total grams fat
300	40	20	5

Bunny Foxhoven, R.D.

Significant source of the following vitamins, minerals and other nutrients:

Vitamins A, C, Thiamin, Riboflavin, Niacin, Potassium, Iron, fiber and Phosphorus

Tacos With a Twist

Ingredients:

1 dozen taco shells
1 lb lean ground turkey or beef
1 8 oz. can chili beans
1 t. chili powder
1 8 oz. can chopped tomatoes
1/2 cup salsa (see recipe)
1/2 small onion, diced
1/2 head iceberg lettuce
2 tomatoes, diced
4 oz. fat free cheddar cheese
1/2 cup nonfat plain yogurt.

Directions:

Brown meat and onion in skillet, add chili beans, chili powder, canned tomatoes, and salsa, heat through. Place 2 T. meat mixture in taco shell top with lettuce, tomato, cheese and yogurt. Makes 12 tacos.

Nutrition Information:

Total calories	Total grams protein	Total grams carbohydrate	Total grams fat
216	6	15	9

Significant source of the following vitamins, minerals and other nutrients:

Vitamins A, C, Thiamin, Riboflavin, Niacin, Potassium, Iron, fiber and Phosphorus

Bunny Foxhoven, R.D.

Mexican Potato Skins

Ingredients:

6 medium potatoes
1 cup salsa
3 oz. fat free cheddar cheese
1/3 cup nonfat plain yogurt

Directions:

Bake potatoes, unwrapped, in oven or microwave until just tender (about 20 minutes in oven or 5 minutes in microwave) Cut in half and using spoon remove middle leaving about 1/2 inch of potato along skin. Spoon on 1/6 cup of salsa and 1/2 oz. cheese. Bake at 375 for 5 minutes or until cheese is bubbly. Top with 1 T. yogurt. Makes 6 potato skins.

Nutrition Information:

Total calories	Total grams protein	Total grams carbohydrate	Total grams fat
188	8	30	3

Significant source of the following vitamins, minerals and other nutrients:

Calcium, Potassium and Iron

Chicken Wonderful

Ingredients:

1 dozen whole wheat flour tortillas or corn tortillas
1 lb. chicken breasts, chopped
2/3 c. non fat plain yogurt
4 oz. non fat sharp cheddar cheese, grated
1 T. fresh cilantro or parsley
2 cloves garlic, minced
1 large onion, chopped
1 16 oz can whole tomatoes, chopped
1 8 oz. can tomato sauce
1 8 oz. can diced green chilies
1/2 t. oregano

Directions:

Sauté onions and garlic in small amount of tomato sauce, add tomatoes, chilies and oregano. Simmer 20 minutes. Mix chicken or turkey, yogurt and cilantro into sauce that is simmering. Layer tortillas then sauce mixture until ingredients are all used. Top with shredded cheese. Bake at 350 for 25 minutes. Serves 12.

Nutrition Information:

Total calories	Total grams protein	Total grams carbohydrate	Total grams fat
195	15	21	6

Significant source of the following vitamins, minerals and other nutrients:

Vitamin C, Niacin, Calcium and Lycopene

Bunny Foxhoven, R.D.

Chicken Fajitas

Ingredients:

4 boneless skinless chicken breasts, cut into strips
8 oz. "Kraft Free" Italian salad dressing
12 whole wheat flour tortillas
1 small onion, cut into strips
medium bell pepper, also cut into strips
16 oz. favorite salsa
8 oz. non fat cheddar cheese
4 oz. nonfat plain yogurt
2 whole tomatoes, chopped
1/2 head lettuce, chopped

Directions:

Cook strips of chicken in small amount of water until tender, add Italian dressing, onion and bell pepper strips and cook until liquid is gone. Place chicken, onions and peppers on tortilla, top with 1 T. yogurt, salsa, cheese, lettuce and tomatoes. Serves 12.

Nutrition Information:

Total calories	Total grams protein	Total grams carbohydrate	Total grams fat
215	18	20	7

Significant source of the following vitamins, minerals and other nutrients:

Vitamin C, Niacin, Potassium, Calcium and Lycopene

Chicken Enchiladas

Ingredients:

1 dozen corn tortillas
1 lb cooked, chopped chicken or ground turkey
2/3 c. nonfat plain yogurt
4 oz nonfat sharp cheddar cheese, grated
1 T. fresh cilantro or parsley
2 garlic cloves, minced
1 large onion, chopped
1 16 oz. can whole tomatoes, chopped
1 8 oz. can tomato sauce
1 8 oz. can diced green chilies
1/2 t. oregano

Directions:

Sauté onions and garlic in small amount on tomato sauce, add tomatoes, chilies and oregano, simmer 20 minutes. Mix chicken or turkey, yogurt and cilantro and 1/2 sauce mixture. Place spoonful of meat mixture in tortilla, roll loosely and place in greased baking dish side by side. Cover with remaining sauce Top with shredded cheese. Bake at 350 for 25 minutes. Serves 12.

Nutrition Information:

Total calories	Total grams protein	Total grams carbohydrate	Total grams fat
175	16	18	5

Significant source of the following vitamins, minerals and other nutrients:

Vitamin C, Thiamin, Riboflavin, Niacin, Potassium, Iron and Lycopene

Bunny Foxhoven, R.D.

Amigo Pie

Corn bread batter ingredients:

1 c. whole wheat pastry flour
1 c. all purpose flour
2 c. corn meal
4 t. baking soda
2 c. skim milk
1 t. salt (optional)
(add 1/3 c. sugar to use as cornbread alone!)

Pie Filling ingredients:

1 32 oz. can chili beans with chili gravy
1 lb. extra lean ground beef
1 t. red chili powder
32 oz. salsa

Directions:

Combine all corn bread batter ingredients and stir to a smooth batter, set aside Brown ground beef in skillet, add chili beans and powder. Place 1/2 corn bread batter in 9 x 13 baking dish that has been greased and floured or sprayed with non stick spray. Pour in meat/bean mixture. Pour remaining batter on top and spread smooth. Bake at 350 for 35 - 40 minutes until cornbread is golden brown and done in the center. Top with salsa. Serves 12.

Nutrition Information:

Total calories	Total grams protein	Total grams carbohydrate	Total grams fat
278	15	40	6

Significant source of the following vitamins, minerals and other nutrients:

Thiamin, Niacin, Potassium and Iron

Bunny Foxhoven, R.D.

Chapter 27
Down Home U.S.A.

1. Spinach Quiche and Pie Crust
2. Cous Cous Chicken Toss
3. Nut Stuffed Chicken Breasts
4. Chicken and Artichokes
5. Baked White Fish and Veggies
6. Snappy Snapper
7. Tasty Tuna Noodle Casserole
8. Lemon Pepper White Fish
9. Turkey Pot Pie
10. Beef Stroganoff
11. Kraut Bidox (Cabbage Burgers)
12. Skinny Gravy
13. Backyard B-B-Q Sauce

Spinach Quiche and Pie Crust

Pie Crust ingredients:

1/2 cup very cold water
1 1/2 cup whole wheat pastry flour
1/8 t. salt
1/4 cup canola margarine
1 1/2 T. oil
(to make a sweet pie crust for desserts add 2 T. sugar or honey)

Quiche ingredients:

1 10 oz. package frozen or fresh spinach
1 cup 1% cottage cheese
1 cup skim buttermilk
1 T. whole wheat pastry flour
6 eggs
1 T. parsley
1 t. basil
1/4 t. pepper
1/4 t. nutmeg
2 T. green onions, sliced

Directions:

To make pie crust, mix dry ingredients, cut margarine into small pieces and add to flour, mix until becomes coarse mealy texture. add oil and 1/3 cup water. Mix until becomes a ball. Add drops of water if it is too dry. Coat ball with flour and place in covered bowl in refrigerator for 2 - 3 hours. Remove dough ball and roll into 1/8th inch circle. Place in oil sprayed and floured pie pan. Shape dough into pan and eliminate all bubbles from under dough. Shape edges using thumbs or fork to create design, cut off all excess dough, partially bake at 350 degrees for 3 - 4 minutes to brown. It is ready to fill and

Bunny Foxhoven, R.D.

bake. To make quiche, cook or thaw spinach and drain well, chop finely. Combine cottage cheese, buttermilk, flour, eggs and spices, mix in spinach and stir well, pour into pie shell and bake for 30 minutes at 375 degrees. Makes 9 slices.

Nutrition Information:

Total calories	Total grams protein	Total grams carbohydrate	Total grams fat
260	6.5	17	18

Significant source of the following vitamins, minerals and other nutrients:
Vitamins A, C, D, Calcium and Iron

Cous Cous Chicken Toss

Ingredients:

6 boneless, skinless chicken breasts, cubed
1 cup carrots, chopped
1/2 cup celery, chopped
1/2 cup cauliflower
2 cups onions, sliced
1/4 cup raisins
1 1/2 cup tomatoes, chopped
2 cups quick cooking couscous
1 cup dry white wine
3 T. slivered almonds
1 t. coriander
1 t. thyme
1/2 t. rosemary
1/2 t. salt
1/2 t. paprika
1 t. cinnamon
1 T. margarine

Directions:

In pan combine chicken, vegetables, wine, thyme, rosemary, salt, paprika and water to boil in. Reduce heat and simmer for 20 minutes. In small pan toast almonds until golden and remove from heat and set aside. Using same pan sauté onion, coriander and raisins in 1 T. water and cook slowly for 5 minutes. Pour all but 1/2 cup of the water from the chicken, add tomatoes and cinnamon and mix well, cook an additional 5 minutes. Combine chicken mixture with raisin mixture and serve it on top of couscous. Serves 10.

Bunny Foxhoven, R.D.

Nutrition Information:

Total calories Total grams protein Total grams carbohydrate Total grams fat
278   18   30   8

Significant source of the following vitamins, minerals and other nutrients:

Vitamins A, C, Niacin, Potassium, Phosphorus and Iron

Nut Stuffed Chicken Breasts

Ingredients:

8 boneless, skinless chicken breasts
1 cups wild rice
1 cup brown rice
1 bouillon cubes
1/2 cup chopped nuts
1 t. parsley
1 t. thyme
1 t. marjoram
1 medium onion, chopped
1/4 cup celery, chopped
1/2 cup fresh mushrooms, chopped
or use 2 packages wild rice plus vegetables to stuff chicken

Directions:

Combine rice and cook according to package but add bouillon cube to boiling water. Sauté onion, celery and mushrooms in small amount of water, add to rice and add spices and nuts. Clean and slice pocket into chicken, stuff rice into pocket. Place in baking dish and cover tightly. Bake at 350 for 30 - 40 minutes until chicken is cooked through.

Nutrition Information:

Total calories	Total grams protein	Total grams carbohydrate	Total grams fat
245	31	15	7

Significant source of the following vitamins, minerals and other nutrients:

Niacin, Potassium, Phosphorus and Iron

Bunny Foxhoven, R.D.

Baked White Fish and Veggies

Ingredients:

2 lb. white fish, flounder, roughy, cod…
1/4 t. pepper
1 onion, finely chopped
1 green pepper, chopped
4 large tomatoes, chopped
1 bay leaf
1 carrot, sliced thin
1 lemon, sliced thin

Directions:

Arrange fish in baking dish, place remaining ingredients around and over fish and top with lemon slices. Bake at 350 degrees for 25 minutes. Makes 4 8 oz servings.

Nutrition Information:

Total calories	Total grams protein	Total grams carbohydrate	Total grams fat
220	27	11	8

Significant source of the following vitamins, minerals and other nutrients:

Vitamin A, C, Niacin, Potassium and Phosphorus

Snappy Snapper

Ingredients:

1 1/2 lb. red snapper
1 large onion, chopped
2 stalks celery, chopped
1/2 lb. mushrooms, chopped
2 T. lemon juice
1 t. Worcestershire sauce

Directions:

Spread vegetables over baking dish and lay fish on top. Pour lemon juice and Worcestershire sauce over and bake at 350 degrees for 20 minutes. Makes 4 6 oz. servings.

Nutrition Information:

Total calories	Total grams protein	Total grams carbohydrate	Total grams fat
257	36	3	11

Significant source of the following vitamins, minerals and other nutrients:

Thiamin, Riboflavin, Potassium, Phosphorus and Iron

Bunny Foxhoven, R.D.

Tasty Tuna Noodle Casserole

Ingredients:

1 7 oz can white tuna in water, drained
1 16 oz pkg. wide egg noodles
1 medium onion, chopped
2 stalks celery, chopped
2 cups sliced mushrooms
2 chicken bouillon cubes
1/2 cup plain non fat yogurt
1/2 cup skim milk
3 T. flour
pinch pepper

Directions:

Boil noodles until tender, drain and rinse. Dissolve flour in milk, Place noodles, milk mixture and all remaining ingredients in large baking dish and bake at 350 for 45 minutes, serve hot, makes 8 1 cup servings.

Nutrition Information:

Total calories	Total grams protein	Total grams carbohydrate	Total grams fat
261	15	43	3

Significant source of the following vitamins, minerals and other nutrients:

Thiamin, Riboflavin, Niacin, Potassium, Phosphorus and Iron

Lemon Pepper White Fish

Ingredients:

3 lb fresh white fish, fillets
1/4 c. lemon juice
1 t. black pepper
1/2 t. fresh garlic or powder
1/4 t. onion powder

Directions:

In shallow baking dish lay fillets out flat. pour lemon juice over fish and sprinkle spices evenly over them. Bake covered for 20 minutes at 350 degrees until fish flakes apart. Serves 8.

Nutrition Information:

Total calories	Total grams protein	Total grams carbohydrate	Total grams fat
216	45	0	4

Significant source of the following vitamins, minerals and other nutrients:

Potassium, Phosphorus and Iron

Bunny Foxhoven, R.D.

Turkey Pot Pie

Ingredients:

Batter
3 egg whites, beaten stiff
1 c. whole wheat pastry flour
1 T baking powder
1/4 t. light salt
1/2 t. sugar
1 c. skim milk
3 egg yolks

Pie Filling
1 medium onion
2 bouillon cubes
1 c. water
1/2 c. skim milk
3 t. flour
1 lb. lean ground turkey (or chicken cut into chunks)
1 c. fresh or frozen peas
1/2 c. chopped celery
1/2 c. chopped carrots
1 medium potato, cubed
4 T. chopped parsley
1/4 t. black pepper
1 t. poultry seasoning

Directions:

Beat egg whites until stiff. Mix dry ingredients in one bowl and wet ingredients in another. Add dry ingredients to wet ingredients. Fold in egg whites. Spread 1/2 batter

Into greased and floured 9 x 13 inch baking dish. Save other half of batter for top of pie. Spread over meat filling at the end. (You may use favorite non sweet pie crust, typical biscuit batter or rolled out refrigerator biscuits for convenience but may reduce nutritional value of recipe)

Prepare Filling: Brown ground turkey, sauté onion and celery, add water and bouillon, simmer. Add flour to cold milk and stir into turkey mixture. add remaining ingredients and heat through. Pour onto bottom crust batter and spread out evenly. Top with remaining batter. Bake at 350 for 35 - 40 minutes or until crust is golden brown and filling is bubbling. Serves 12.

Nutrition Information:

Total calories	Total grams protein	Total grams carbohydrate	Total grams fat
184	15	16	6

Significant source of the following vitamins, minerals and other nutrients:

Vitamin A, Potassium, Phosphorus and Iron

Bunny Foxhoven, R.D.

Beef Stroganoff

Ingredients:

1 lb. lean ground beef, or cubed sirloin or flank steak.
16 oz. package egg noodles or 4 cups cooked brown rice
8 oz. non fat plain yogurt
1 medium onion
1/2 cup mushrooms, sliced
1/4 t. pepper
1/2 cup whole wheat pastry flour
1 bouillon cube
1 c. water

Directions:

Brown beef in skillet, sauté onions with beef, sprinkle flour over meat and coat thoroughly, stir in bouillon and water to make gravy. Add mushrooms. Mix in yogurt and remove from heat immediately to prevent separation. Serve over boiled noodles or rice. Serves 8.

Nutrition Information:

Total calories	Total grams protein	Total grams carbohydrate	Total grams fat
269	17	26	10

Significant source of the following vitamins, minerals and other nutrients:

Thiamin, Riboflavin, Niacin, Phosphorus and Iron

Kraut Bidox Cabbage Burgers)

Ingredients:

1 package Rhodes whole wheat bread dough
2 head green cabbage
2 lb. lean ground beef
1/2 t. garlic powder
1/2 t. salt (optional)
1/2 t. pepper

Directions:

Thaw frozen bread dough, cut each loaf into 6 wedges. flatten and roll into 8 inch circles.

Brown the ground beef in skillet, drain and rinse to remove all fat. Chop cabbage and boil to tender in 3 qts water, drain.

Mix cabbage beef and spices together, Place 1/2 cup mixture onto flattened dough and pull edges up and pinch together. Place on lightly greased cookie sheet and bake at 350 for 20 - 30 minutes until dough is golden brown.

Makes 18.

Nutrition Information:

Total calories	Total grams protein	Total grams carbohydrate	Total grams fat
283	30	25	7

Significant source of the following vitamins, minerals and other nutrients:

Vitamin A, Thiamin, Riboflavin, Niacin and Iron

Bunny Foxhoven, R.D.

Skinny Gravy

Ingredients:

2 cups broth or fat free meat drippings (hint.. pour all drippings into large cup or bowl, chill, remove all hard fat that has risen to top)
pinch black pepper
1/2 t. onion powder
pinch salt, thyme, sage, marjoram and basil each (use any or all of these spices for added flavor)
1 cup skim milk
5 T. flour

Directions:

   Heat broth and spices in large sauce pan, simmer 5 minutes. Dissolve flour in cold skim milk, slowly add milk and flour paste to broth mixture stirring constantly until mixture thickens. Turn heat to very low and cook 8 - 10 minutes until desired thickness. Makes 3 cups gravy.

Nutrition Information:

Total calories	Total grams protein	Total grams carbohydrate	Total grams fat
19	1	4	0

Significant source of the following vitamins, minerals and other nutrients:
0

A Parent's Guide to Sports Nutrition for Young Athletes

Backyard BBQ Sauce

Ingredients:

1 16 oz. can whole peeled tomatoes, diced
3 T. onion, chopped
1/4 t. basil
1/2 t. garlic, minced
1 T. lemon juice
1 T. brown sugar or molasses
1/2 t. Worcestershire sauce
1/4 t. chili powder
1/2 pepper

Directions:

Combine all ingredients and simmer for five minutes. Use on any fresh lean meat. Makes 1 cup

Nutrition Information:

Total calories	Total grams protein	Total grams carbohydrate	Total grams fat
33	.5	7	0

Significant source of the following vitamins, minerals and other nutrients:

Vitamin C

Chapter 28

Veggies and Then Some

1. Green Beans and Ham
2. Easy Cheesy Broccoli
3. Candied Sweet Potatoes
4. Stuffed Zucchini
5. Confetti Cabbage
6. Grandmas Green Bean and Sausage Casserole
7. Zucchini Medley
8. Quick Broccoli Soufflé

Green Beans and Ham

Ingredients:

1 lb. fresh green beans, cut and washed
1 cup water
2 beef bouillon cubes dissolved in water
1 medium onion, chopped
1/3 cup lean ham, chopped
3/4 t. salt
1/4 t. pepper

Directions:

Prepare green beans, combine all ingredients and bring to boil, reduce heat and simmer for 25 minutes. Makes 6 1/2 cup servings.

Nutrition Information:

Total calories	Total grams protein	Total grams carbohydrate	Total grams fat
46	4	4	1

Significant source of the following vitamins, minerals and other nutrients:

Thiamin, Riboflavin and Niacin

Bunny Foxhoven, R.D.

Easy Cheesy Broccoli

Ingredients:

1 lb. fresh broccoli, chopped or speared
4 oz. nonfat cheddar cheese, shredded
1/4 cup skim milk

Directions:

Steam broccoli to desired tenderness. Microwave cheese and milk to melt cheese, stir often. Pour over broccoli and serve. Makes 4 4 oz. servings.

Nutrition Information:

Total calories	Total grams protein	Total grams carbohydrate	Total grams fat
103	10	4	5

Significant source of the following vitamins, minerals and other nutrients:

Vitamins A, C, and Calcium

Candied Sweet Potatoes

Ingredients:

2 1/2 lb sweet potatoes
1/3 c. brown sugar
2 T. orange juice (not concentrated)

Directions:

Boil and peel potatoes, cut into 2 "chunks and place into baking dish. Add sugar and e.g. Bake at 350 degrees for 20 minutes. Makes 6 1/2 c. servings.

Nutrition Information:

Total calories	Total grams protein	Total grams carbohydrate	Total grams fat
114	1	25	0

Significant source of the following vitamins, minerals and other nutrients:

Vitamins A, C and Potassium

Bunny Foxhoven, R.D.

Stuffed Zucchini

Ingredients:

4 6 inch long zucchini
1 small onion, sliced thin
1 green pepper, diced
1/2 cup tomatoes, diced
1 c. tomato juice
1 clove garlic, minced
1 t. oregano
1 piece whole wheat bread, dried or toasted

Directions:

Cut zucchini lengthwise and scoop out center, combine center pulp with remaining ingredients except 1/4 cup tomato juice. Sauté vegetables until soft. Arrange zucchini in baking dish, place cooked vegetables in zucchini shells and top with remaining tomato juice, Crumble toast and sprinkle on to of zucchini. Bake at 350 degrees for 30 minutes. Spoon juices from bottom of pan over zucchini before serving. Makes 6 servings.

To make this a main dish add 1 lb. ground turkey sausage to vegetables!

Nutrition Information:

Total calories	Total grams protein	Total grams carbohydrate	Total grams fat
44	2	8	0

Significant source of the following vitamins, minerals and other nutrients:

Vitamins A, C and Potassium

Grandmas Green Bean and Sausage Casserole

Ingredients:

1 s. spaghetti sauce
2 24 oz. cans green bean, drained
1/2 lb. turkey Italian sausage, browned

Directions:

Combine all ingredients in baking dish, bake at 350 degrees for 25 minutes. Makes 6 1/2 c. servings.

Nutrition Information:

Total calories	Total grams protein	Total grams carbohydrate	Total grams fat
155	12	11	7

Significant source of the following vitamins, minerals and other nutrients:

Vitamin C, Riboflavin, Niacin, Potassium, Phosphorus Iron and Lycopene

Bunny Foxhoven, R.D.

Zucchini Medley

Ingredients:

3 cups zucchini, chopped
1 small eggplant
2 medium green peppers, chopped
1 onion, chopped
1 clove of fresh garlic, minced
2 large tomatoes, chopped
1/4 t. pepper

Directions:

Combine all ingredients and cook covered on low for 20 minutes. Uncover and cook on medium heat for 15 minutes more, stirring occasionally. Makes 4 1 c. servings.

Nutrition Information:

Total calories	Total grams protein	Total grams carbohydrate	Total grams fat
201	24	8	7

Significant source of the following vitamins, minerals and other nutrients:

Vitamins A, C, Riboflavin, Potassium, Calcium and Lycopene

Quick Broccoli Soufflé

Ingredients:

2 c. broccoli, chopped
1 onion, chopped
12 egg whites, beaten stiff
1/2 c. skim milk
1/2 c. grated parmesan cheese
1/4 t. pepper
1/2 t. garlic powder

Directions:

Sauté onion and Broccoli in small amount of water in non stick pan. In bowl combine egg whites, and spices, add milk and beat again, pour over broccoli and onions and cook over medium heat until bottom begins to brown sprinkle with cheese and cook on low heat until becomes firm enough to cut into wedges and serve. Makes 4 servings.

Nutrition Information:

Total calories	Total grams protein	Total grams carbohydrate	Total grams fat
201	24	8	7

Significant source of the following vitamins, minerals and other nutrients:

Vitamins A, C, Riboflavin, Potassium and Calcium

Bunny Foxhoven, R.D.

Chapter 29

Best Bakery

1. Apple Oat Bran Muffins
2. Fruit and Fiber Muffins
3. Wholesome Oat Bran Muffins
4. French Toast Sticks
5. Oatmeal Pancakes
6. Chewy Granola Bars
7. Soft Pretzels
8. Great Whole Wheat Bagels
9. Oatmeal Bread
10. Tasty Corn Bread

Apple Oat Bran Muffins

Ingredients:

1 1/2 cups oat bran
1/2 c. whole wheat pastry flour
3 T. brown sugar
2 t. baking powder
1/2 t. salt
1 t. cinnamon
1/2 c. apple juice
1/4 c. skim milk
1 egg
1 T. vegetable oil
2 T. honey
1 cup apples, diced
2 T. raisins

Directions:

Mix all liquid ingredients in 1 bowl and dry ingredients in another. Add dry plus apples and raisins to liquid ingredients, mix only until just moistened. Fill lined muffin tin and bake at 400 for 20 minutes. Makes 12 muffins.

Nutrition Information:

Total calories	Total grams protein	Total grams carbohydrate	Total grams fat
148	3	34	2

Significant source of the following vitamins, minerals and other nutrients:

Vitamin C, Thiamin, Riboflavin, Niacin and Calcium

Bunny Foxhoven, R.D.

Fruit and Fiber Muffins

Ingredients:

1/2 cup orange juice
1 c. dried fruit (apricot, raisins, apples, pineapple or dates)
1/4 cup brown sugar
1 cup oat bran
1/4 cup wheat germ
3/4 cup whole wheat pastry flour
2 t. baking powder
1/2 cup skim milk
2 eggs

Directions:

Mix dry ingredients in one bowl and liquid plus fruit ingredients in another. Add dry ingredients to wet and stir until just moistened. Fill lined muffin tins and bake for 15 minutes at 400. Makes 12 muffins.

Nutrition Information:

Total calories	Total grams protein	Total grams carbohydrate	Total grams fat
102	4	21	1

Significant source of the following vitamins, minerals and other nutrients:

Vitamin A, Thiamin, Riboflavin, Niacin and Calcium

Wholesome Oat Bran Muffins

Ingredients:

2 1/4 c. oat bran
1/4 cup brown sugar
1/4 cup chopped walnuts (optional)
1/4 cup raisins or other dried fruits
1 T/ baking powder
1/2 t. salt
3/4 cup skim milk
2 eggs
1/4 c. honey

Directions:

Mix all ingredients, stir until just moistened. Fill lined muffin tin and bake 425 for 15 minutes or until golden brown. Makes 12 muffins.
Nutrition Information:

Total calories Total grams protein Total grams carbohydrate Total grams fat
112   6   22   3

Significant source of the following vitamins, minerals and other nutrients:

Vitamin C, Thiamin, Riboflavin, Niacin, Fiber and Calcium

Bunny Foxhoven, R.D.

French Toast Sticks

Ingredients:

3 egg whites plus 2 whole eggs
or
3 whole eggs
1/2 cup skim milk
1 t. cinnamon
8 slices whole wheat toast

Directions:

Mix eggs, milk and cinnamon until smooth in shallow bowl. Dip bread one slice at a time on both sides and place on 350 degree griddle. cook until golden brown, flip and cook other side. Cut into 4 sticks. Dip into syrup or fruit jam in small cups. Makes 8 slices or 32 sticks.

Nutrition Information:

Total calories	Total grams protein	Total grams carbohydrate	Total grams fat
103	6	14	2

Significant source of the following vitamins, minerals and other nutrients:

Thiamin, Riboflavin, Niacin and Fiber

Oatmeal Pancakes

Ingredients:

1 1/2 cup oatmeal
3/4 cup flour (whole wheat for buckwheat flavor)
1 T. sugar
1 t. baking soda
1 egg
1 T. oil
2 cups skim milk or buttermilk

Directions:

Combine all ingredients and mix lightly, will be slightly lumpy, let stand for 15 minutes. heat non-stick griddle. Pour 1/4 cup onto griddle, bake until bubbles form and begin to pop, turn and cook other side. Serve with light syrup or fruit jam. Makes 12 4 inch pancakes.

Nutrition Information:

Total calories	Total grams protein	Total grams carbohydrate	Total grams fat
112	5	20	1

Significant source of the following vitamins, minerals and other nutrients:

Thiamin, Riboflavin, Niacin and Fiber

Bunny Foxhoven, R.D.

Chewy Granola Bars

Ingredients:

2 cups rolled oats
2/3 cup brown sugar
1/2 cup unsalted peanuts
1/2 cup wheat germ
1/2 cup raisins
2 eggs
1 t. vanilla

Directions:

Combine all ingredients and press into 9 x 9 inch baking dish and bake at 350 degrees for 30 minutes, let cool and cut into 16 bars. Substitute other dried fruits and nuts for flavors.

Nutrition Information:

Total calories	Total grams protein	Total grams carbohydrate	Total grams fat
82	2	12	3

Significant source of the following vitamins, minerals and other nutrients:

Thiamin, Riboflavin, Niacin and Fiber

Soft Pretzels

Ingredients:

1 loaf whole wheat bread dough (see recipe) or use frozen, thawed
1 egg white, beaten with 1 t. water
3 T. salt or sesame seeds

Directions:

Thaw dough and cover and let rise in warm place until doubled. Divide into 12 pieces. roll into long snakes and shape into pretzel twist. Preheat oven to 400 degrees. Bring 2 inches of water to boil in skillet and let cook until rise to surface. Brush lightly with egg and sprinkle with salt or seeds. Bake at 400 degrees for 18 minutes or until brown. Makes 12 pretzels.

Nutrition Information:

Total calories	Total grams protein	Total grams carbohydrate	Total grams fat
110	3	18	2

Significant source of the following vitamins, minerals and other nutrients:

Thiamin, Riboflavin, Niacin and Fiber

Bunny Foxhoven, R.D.

Great Whole Wheat Bagels

Ingredients:

1 T. active dry yeast
3 T. sugar
1 cup warm water
1 1/2 cups whole wheat pastry flour
1 1/2 cups unbleached white flour
1 t. salt
1/2 cup raisins, blueberries, or other dried fruits or nuts
2 t. cinnamon

Directions:

   Mix yeast, sugar and warm water in large bowl and let proof. Mix in flours and salt, knead 10 minutes or in food processor for 15 seconds until smooth and elastic. Add more flour if necessary. Cover with moist towel and let rise in warm place for 40 minutes. Punch down and shape into 5 inch long x 3/4 inch wide tubes. Pinch into circle to make bagel shape. Prepare large pot with water and bring to boil. Preheat oven to 350. Drop bagels into boiling water a few at a time, as they rise to top remove and place on cookie sheet sprayed with vegetable spray. when all bagels are boiled bake in oven for 10 minutes. Raise heat to 400 and bake another 10 minutes. Makes 12 bagels.

Nutrition Information:

Total calories	Total grams protein	Total grams carbohydrate	Total grams fat
148	5	33	1

Significant source of the following vitamins, minerals and other nutrients:

Vitamin A, Thiamin, Riboflavin, Niacin and Fiber

Bunny Foxhoven, R.D.

Oatmeal Bread

Ingredients:

1 cup water
1 cup rolled oats
2 T. honey
1 T. margarine
1 t. salt
1 T. active dry yeast
1/2 t. sugar
1/3 cup warm water
1 1/2 cup whole wheat pastry flour
1 cup unbleached white flour

Directions:

In small pan boil water, add oats, honey, margarine and salt, let cool. In large bowl combine yeast sugar and warm water. Let it proof. Add 1 cup of each flour to yeast mixture plus cooled oat mixture and begin kneading. Add flour as necessary, kneed until smooth and elastic. Approximately 10 minutes kneading or 15 seconds in a food processor! Place in large bowl sprayed with vegetable spray and cover with a moist towel. Place in warm area (oven on lowest setting) for 1 hour until rises to double size. Punch down center and shape into loaf and place in loaf baking pan. Cover with moist towel and let rise again in pan in warm oven. Remove and heat oven to 350, remove towel and bake for 45 minutes or until golden brown. Makes 16 1/2 inch slices.

Nutrition Information:

Total calories	Total grams protein	Total grams carbohydrate	Total grams fat
102	4	20	1

Significant source of the following vitamins, minerals and other nutrients:

Thiamin, Riboflavin, Niacin and Fiber

Bunny Foxhoven, R.D.

Tasty Corn Bread

Ingredients:

1 c. whole wheat pastry flour
1 c. cornmeal
2 T. sugar
4 T. baking powder
1/4 t. salt
1 c. skim milk
1 egg
2 T. vegetable oil
Optional: you can add 2 T. diced green chilies (you decide the hotness)

Directions:

Combine dry ingredients in 1 bowl and wet ingredients in another. pour wet into dry and stir until blended. Pour into a 9 x 9 inch nonstick baking dish and bake at 375 for 25 minutes. Makes 8 pieces.

Nutrition Information:

Total calories	Total grams protein	Total grams carbohydrate	Total grams fat
117	4	19	3

Significant source of the following vitamins, minerals and other nutrients:

Thiamin, Riboflavin, Niacin and Fiber

A Parent's Guide to Sports Nutrition for Young Athletes

Chapter 30

Sinless Desserts

1. Tropical Fruit Salad Colada
2. Fruit Sorbet
3. Fruit Ice Cream Popsicles
4. Oatmeal Raisin Cookies
5. Devilish Chocolate Cake
6. Chocolate Angel Food Cake
7. Non Fat Cherry Cheesecake
8. Carrot Zucchini Bars

Bunny Foxhoven, R.D.

Tropical Fruit Salad Colada

Ingredients:

1/4 c. shredded coconut
1 c. nonfat fruit flavored yogurt, preferably banana
1/4 c. pineapple juice
1 c. banana, chopped
1 c. pineapple, chopped
1 c. oranges, chopped
1 c. any other tropical fruit, ie. kiwi, guava, papaya…

Directions:

Combine yogurt, coconut, juice and fold over fruit lightly, and serve. Makes 4 1 c. servings.

Nutrition Information:

Total calories	Total grams protein	Total grams carbohydrate	Total grams fat
211	4	46	2

Significant source of the following vitamins, minerals and other nutrients:

Vitamins A, C, Thiamin, Riboflavin, Niacin and Fiber

Fruit Sorbet

Ingredients:

3/4 cup water
1 small package plain gelatin
2 egg whites
2 10 oz. packages frozen berries (any)
1 banana, sliced
2/3 cup apple juice concentrate (no sugar added preferably)

Directions:

Pour gelatin into pan with cold water and heat over low heat to dissolve. In bowl whip egg whites to stiff, stir into gelatin and cook 4 minutes until thick. In blender puree fruit and apple juice. Add egg mixture and pour into bowl and freeze 1 hour.

Mix or blenderize until smooth and return to bowl and freezer until solid. Serve topped with fresh berries. Makes 1 quart.

Nutrition Information:

Total calories	Total grams protein	Total grams carbohydrate	Total grams fat
109	2	25	0

Significant source of the following vitamins, minerals and other nutrients:

Vitamins A, C and Fiber

Bunny Foxhoven, R.D.

Fruit Ice Cream Popsicles

Ingredients:

6 oz. frozen orange juice concentrate
6 oz. frozen pineapple juice concentrate
3 1/2 c. skim milk
6 whole oranges, peeled and seeded

Directions:

Blend in high speed blender until smooth. Place in ice cube trays and freeze for 2 hours. remove and blend again until soft. Refreeze in ice cube trays with popsicle sticks or in small containers and eat like ice cream. Makes 12 popsicles.

Nutrition Information:

Total calories	Total grams protein	Total grams carbohydrate	Total grams fat
99	4	22	0

Significant source of the following vitamins, minerals and other nutrients:

Vitamins A, C, Calcium and Fiber

Oatmeal Raisin Cookies

Ingredients:

3 cups rolled oats
1 cup whole wheat pastry flour
1 t. salt
1 t. baking powder
1 t. cinnamon
1/2 cup raisins, carob chips, dates or other dried fruits
1/4 cup melted margarine
3/4 cup brown sugar, packed
2 eggs
1/2 cup plain nonfat yogurt
1 t. vanilla extract

Directions:

Mix dry ingredients in one bowl and wet ingredients in another. Slowly add dry to wet ingredients and mix until creamy. Drop by spoonfuls onto greased cookie sheet and bake 12 to 15 minutes at 350. Makes 4 dozen small or 2 dozen large cookies.

Nutrition Information:

Total calories	Total grams protein	Total grams carbohydrate	Total grams fat
114	3	19	3

Significant source of the following vitamins, minerals and other nutrients:

Thiamin, Riboflavin, Niacin and Fiber

Bunny Foxhoven, R.D.

Devilish Chocolate Cake

Ingredients:

Cake:

1 cup sugar
2 cups whole wheat pastry flour
1/2 cup skim buttermilk
2 egg whites
1 egg yolk
1 t. vanilla
3 T. cocoa powder
3 T. margarine
1 cup water
1 t. baking soda
1 t. baking powder

Frosting:

3 T. margarine
3 T. cocoa powder
1 t. vanilla
1 1/2 powdered sugar
1 T. skim milk

Directions:

Cake:

Boil 1 cup water and pour into large mixing bowl, melt margarine in water, add cocoa powder, sugar, vanilla, and egg yolk, stir until smooth. Begin adding baking soda, buttermilk, flour an buttermilk and mix well. Whip egg whites to stiff stage and fold into batter. Pour into greased and floured baking pan and bake at 350 for 45 minutes. Cool and frost.

Frosting:

Mix all ingredients well, adding milk last, if too dry add more milk, if too wet add more sugar. frost cake.

Nutrition Information: Without Frosting

Total calories Total grams protein Total grams carbohydrate Total grams fat
175   4   32   4

Significant source of the following vitamins, minerals and other nutrients:

Thiamin, Riboflavin, Niacin and Fiber

Nutrition Information: With Frosting

Total calories Total grams protein Total grams carbohydrate Total grams fat
263   5   49   7

Significant source of the following vitamins, minerals and other nutrients:

Thiamin, Riboflavin, Niacin and Fiber

Bunny Foxhoven, R.D.

Chocolate Angel Food Cake

Ingredients:

3/4 cup pastry flour (this time whole wheat won't work)
1/4 cup cocoa powder
1 1/4 cup sugar
10 egg whites
1 t. cream of tartar
1 t. vanilla
1/2 t. almond extract

Directions:

Mix together flour and cocoa in one bowl, in another whip egg whites until foamy, add cream of tartar and whip to stiff stage. Fold in sugar, spices and flour in small amounts. Pour into ungreased bundt ban and bake for 45 minutes until golden. Let cool in pan on wire rack up side down. Makes 12 slices.

Nutrition Information:

Total calories   Total grams protein   Total grams carbohydrate   Total grams fat
129   4   28   0

Significant source of the following vitamins, minerals and other nutrients:

Not a significant source of nutrients.

Non Fat Cherry Cheesecake

Ingredients:

1 8 oz package Kraft "Philly Free" cream cheese
1/2 c. sugar
1 t. vanilla
1 12 oz can cherries, undrained
1 T. corn starch
1 premade graham cracker crust.

Directions:

Pour cherries and cornstarch into small sauce pan and mix thoroughly, place on low heat and stir slowly until begins to thicken, remove from heat and set aside to cool. In bowl mix cream cheese, sugar and vanilla until smooth. spread into graham cracker crust and top with cooled cherry mixture. Place in refrigerator to set. Makes 8 servings.

Nutrition Information:

Total calories	Total grams protein	Total grams carbohydrate	Total grams fat
163	5	33	1.5

Significant source of the following vitamins, minerals and other nutrients:

Vitamins A, C, Thiamin, Riboflavin, Niacin and Fiber

Bunny Foxhoven, R.D.

Carrot Zucchini Bars

Ingredients:

2 cups whole wheat pastry flour
1 cup zucchini, grated
1 cup carrots, grated
1/2 t. salt
2 eggs
1/2 cup sugar
2 t. grated orange peel
2 t. baking powder
2 t. cinnamon
1 1/2 T. margarine
1 cup chopped nuts

Directions:

Preheat oven to 350 degrees. Grease and flour 9 x 13 inch baking dish. In one bowl mix all dry ingredients. In another bowl mix margarine, eggs, sugar and orange peel until fluffy. Slowly mix in dry ingredients, and beat until blended, stir in zucchini, carrots and nuts. Spread into pan, bake 35 minutes until golden. Cut into bars and cool on rack. Makes 24 bars.

Nutrition Information:

Total calories	Total grams protein	Total grams carbohydrate	Total grams fat
108	4	5	5

Significant source of the following vitamins, minerals and other nutrients:

Vitamins A, C, Thiamin, Riboflavin, Niacin and Fiber

References

1. Bar-Or, Oded, Nutrition for Child and Adolescent Athletes. Sports Science Exchange Vol. 13, #2 2000, Gatorade Sports Science Institute.

2. P.G. Cooper (ed), and AFAA, 1987, Aerobics Theory and Practice (Costa Mesa,, CA: HDL Communications).

3. Coleman, Ellen, R.D. Sports Drink Update, Sports Science Exchange #5 Vol 1, 1988, Gatorade Sports Science Institute.

4. Carey, Ruth, R.D., L.D. Tips for Parents: Food and Drink for the Young Athlete. Sports Science Exchange #2 Vol. 13, 2000, Gatorade Sports Science Institute.

5. Lamb, David R., PhD., FACSM and Shehata, Adel Helmy, Phd, Benefits and Limitations of Pre-hydration Sports Science Exchange Vol. 12, #2 1999, Gatorade Sports Science Institute.

6. Anderson, Dibble, Turkki, Mitchell, Rynbergen, Nutrition in Health and Disease, 17th ed. J. B. Lippencott Company., Philadelphia, Toronto 1982.

7. Williams MH. Nutrition for Fitness and Sport, 4th ed. Dubuque: Brown and Benchmark 1995.

8. Pascoe D.D., E.L. Costal, W.J. Fink, R.A. Roberts, and J.J. Zachwieja (1993) Glycogen resynthesis in skeletal muscle following resistance exercise. Med. Sci Sports Exercise 25:349-354.

9. Layman, D.D. et al, Exercise and Nutrition. Eating proper foods at right time after exercise can speed recovery. July 1999 www.news.uiuc.edu:16080/archives/99.07/exerciseatstip.html

10. Maternal and Infant Nutrition Briefs. Jan/Feb 1996.

11. Walberg Rankin, Janet., PhD., Glycemic Index and Exercise Metabolism Sports Science Exchange. Vol. 10, #1 1997, Gatorade Sports Science Institute.

12. Nutrition Action Health letter 1996.

13. Youth in sports Nutritional Needs, Sports Science Exchange Roundtable #30 1997.

14. Nutrition Perspectives Vol. 21 #1 Jan/Feb 1996.

15. USDA Nutrient database for Standard Reference (release 14)

16. The American Heart Association and the USDA release How to Read the Food Label

17. World Health Organization 1985

18. Leaf, A. and Frisa, K.B. Eating for health or for Athletic Performance. Am. Journal of Clin. Nutr. 49: 1066-1069, 1989.

19. Lemon, P.W. Is More Protein Necessary or Beneficial for Individuals with Physically Active Lifestyles? Nutr. Rev. 54: 5169 - 5175, 1996.

20. R.D. Rosato, fitness for Wellness, 3rd ed. Minn, Mn: West Publishing Co., 1994.

21. C.B. Corbin & R. Lindsey, Concepts of Physical Fitness, 7th ed. Dubuque, Ia: Wm C. Brown Pub., 1991

About the Author

Bunny Foxhoven, RD is a sports nutrition specialist in Denver, Colorado. She works with athletes from the recreational to competitive ranks and has done extensive work with child athletes. She knows how demanding youth sports can be on children's growing bodies and how difficult it can be for parents to provide healthy meals for their children. She is also a competitive cyclist and enjoys mountain biking, water skiing, hiking and playing team sports.

Printed in the United States
24699LVS00003B/64-510